PRAISE
THREE FUNERALS

"*Three Funerals for My Father* is the powerful story of a family's journey from Vietnam to Canada, lyrically told in three distinct voices. It is at once a heart-wrenching memoir and a reckoning of sorts—an unflinching view of the peril and terrible costs to one family making a journey as refugees to an unfamiliar land, uncertain of their welcome . . . Intimate and unforgettable." K.C. DYER, author of *An Accidental Odyssey*

"Jolie Phuong Hoang takes us to a largely forgotten world where many people paid the ultimate price for freedom, the dream of the powerless both then and now. Her family's quest for a better tomorrow is inspiring, daring and brave. A beautifully written story full of love, drama, tears, agony and hope. This is a must-read that celebrates the resilience of the human spirit." HASSAN AL KONTAR, author of *Man at the Airport*

PRAISE FOR *ANCHORLESS*

NORTH STREET BOOK PRIZE, WINNER (2020)
"The book successfully straddles fiction and memoir; there is a haunting magical realism to the writing that creates a dual sense of reality/unreality. This heightens the tension and evokes strong emotions in the reader. . . I am awed at how much horror, beauty, and joy Jolie Hoang packed into those pages." JUDGE, LITERARY FICTION

WISHING SHELF BOOK AWARDS, BRONZE MEDAL (2020)
"Superbly written, this is original in every way. I dare you not to enjoy it. A bronze medal winner and highly recommended."

JUDGE, NON-FICTION

THREE FUNERALS FOR MY FATHER

Three Funerals for My Father

Love, Loss and Escape from Vietnam

JOLIE PHUONG HOANG

TIDEWATER
PRESS

Published by Tidewater Press
New Westminster, BC, Canada
tidewaterpress.ca

978-1-990160-04-2 (print)
978-1-990160-05-9 (e-book)

LIBRARY AND ARCHIVES CANADA CATALOGUING IN PUBLICATION

Title: Three funerals for my father : love, loss and escape from Vietnam / Jolie Phuong Hoang.
Names: Hoang, Jolie Phuong, author.
Identifiers: Canadiana (print) 20210281448 | Canadiana (ebook) 20210281553 | ISBN 9781990160042
(softcover) | ISBN 9781990160059 (HTML)
Subjects: LCSH: Hoang, Jolie Phuong. | LCSH: Hoang, Jolie Phuong—Family. | LCSH: Boat people—
Vietnam—Biography. | LCSH: Refugees—Vietnam—Biography. | LCSH: Refugees—Indonesia—Biography. |
LCSH: Refugees—Canada—Biography. | LCSH: Vietnam—History—1975- | LCGFT: Autobiographies. |
LCGFT: Biographies.
Classification: LCC HV640.5.V5 H63 2021 | DDC 305.8959/22071092—dc23

Several chapters of this book first appeared as *Anchorless*
978-1-525559-1-05 (Hardcover)
978-1-525559-1-12 (Paperback)
978-1-525559-1-29 (ebook)

Front Cover Illustration: Christie Hoang Thuong
Back and Interior Illustrations: Charlotte Nhu Thuong

Printed in Canada

For my father, Hoàng Trọng Phụ, with love and respect,
For my dearest sister, Hoàng Thị Lan Phương—
it took me thirty years to accept our fates.
And for my mother, Võ Thị Sĩ, with love and admiration
for your many years of enduring love and loneliness.
This book is written for you, for many unsaid words, for many
untold stories and for a lifetime of lost times.

NOTES

Prefixes used when addressing family members to show respect and love:

    "Ông" for elder men
    "Bà" for elder women
    "Chú" for an uncle
    "Thím" for the wife of an uncle
    "Chị" for older sister
    "Anh" for older brother
    "Em" for a younger sister or brother

"Hai" is the nickname for the firstborn child in a family—Anh Hai or Chị Hai.

"Út" is the affectionate nickname for the youngest child in a family.

Huế

Quảng Đức

Nha Trang
Đà Lạt ●
● Phan Rang

Saigon/
Ho Chi Minh City
● Mũi Né

Cần Thơ ●
Vũng Tàu

● Cà Mau

● Côn Sơn Island

CONTENTS

I AM HOME

My beloved children! Open the door for me. I am home!
Các con ơi, Ba đã về nhà rồi, mở cửa cho Ba!
Simple sentences that I often wish
I could hear again from my father.
His gentle voice, saying he is home
Simple words, but full of hope.
Simple sentences, but full of love.
Simply telling me to open the door for him.
How many times have I longed to open it?
I turn the page. I am opening the door.

CHAPTER 1

MY FIRST FUNERAL

I died on June 15, 1985, when I was fifty-nine years old. My death was not natural. I died escaping Vietnam with my wife and my three younger children, hoping to reunite with my six older children who were living in Canada, halfway around the world. I died in the Pacific Ocean, trying to shorten the distance between us all.

My soul arrived at the door of Heaven. I knelt in front of God. "Please allow me to postpone my entrance."

God showed me the Book of Heaven. "Your name is written right here. It is your time to walk through this door. Hurry, it is about to close."

I begged God, "Let me live as a ghost. Let the dead stay with the living. Let my soul stay with my children."

"Why would you want more suffering?" God asked. "In Heaven, you are free of the living, at eternal peace. Give me one good reason to let you live as a ghost."

"When I died," I replied, "I could still hear my children's cries. I hear the tears in their hearts. I will do anything for my wife and our children, God. Please, I beg you to let my soul live on as a ghost."

"Is my Heaven meaningless to you? Death comes when your physical being can no longer endure pain. It is a relief to be done with your time on earth. It is time for your tired soul to rest. Why would you want to prolong your agony?"

God seemed puzzled. "It is strange to hear such a request. What can you do for your wife and your children with your helpless soul? Living as a ghost, you will still have your memories but will not be able to talk. You will want to forget, but you will remember. You will feel, but touch will be impossible. You will want to cry but will have no tears. You will be present only to yourself, invisible to the living, caught between life and death."

God paused to listen and heard the anguished cries of my surviving children, my dead children, my wife, my mother, my dead father, my grandchildren, my brothers, my sisters and my friends. God realized that, in death, I was still suffering and stopped lecturing me.

"I still cannot accept being taken away from my wife and my children."

"Perhaps you need to find the answers on your own." God granted my wish and released my soul.

I rushed to Côn Sơn Island, near where the boat sank, to the site where the communist government imprisoned those who tried to escape their own country and were captured at sea. Before the fall of Saigon in 1975, the South Vietnamese government used the island to incarcerate notorious criminals and to torture communists. Many communists or citizens who were accused of being communists were executed or murdered. There were more prisons on this island than homes, more nameless graves than those with tombstones, and many mass graves waiting to be discovered. Côn Sơn Island was home to many ghosts of the present and the past. I heard the weary cries of those who had died unjust deaths and those who died fighting to liberate South Vietnam. Their souls longed for the living to come to this island, to discover and collect their corpses. They dreamed of proper burial ceremonies, close to their living families. The spirits of the dead suffered in agony; the living endured in misery.

I found my wife and my two young sons. They were lying on a

dirty mat in a filthy cell with many other prisoners. I recognized some of them—they were my fellow escapees. My wife wept silently. My sons tried to comfort their mother even as tears dripped from the corners of their own eyes.

"Where is Lan Phương?" I asked my wife. "Phố and Phấn, Father is here. I am right beside you," I screamed, then realized they could not see or hear me. I crumbled to the ground.

Then I heard the familiar voice of our youngest daughter. "Father, is that you?"

"Lan Phương!" I hugged her and she wrapped her arms around me. She could feel me. We felt each other. Then I understood that she was just like me—a ghost with a confused soul that could not rise to Heaven.

"Father, where were you? What happened to us?" asked Lan Phương, her voice trembling.

I held her tiny hands. Our souls flew to the place on the sea where the boat had gone down. Our souls sank under the water and found dead bodies still trapped in the hull, other corpses slowly rising to the surface. We saw miserable souls clinging to their lifeless, drifting bodies. We heard the wails of other anguished ghosts, desperately searched for their remains. We avoided the chaos and sat on a piece of debris, our weightless souls floating on angry waves under a dark purple sky.

"Father, why are we here?"

"Út," I said, using the affectionate term for a youngest child, "we both died from drowning. I am so very sorry I could not save you. Somehow my body is on land, and yours is floating somewhere in this ocean."

She turned and gave me a gentle smile. "But we are still together!"

"We are together in death."

As she started to understand, I could no longer see her clearly.

Her voice faded and her words became indistinct. She let go of my
hand.

I tried to grasp her arm. "Lan Phương, please stay with me! Don't
leave me alone!" But she could not hear me. Then I could see her no
more.

I returned to the island and found my body on the beach, above
the tideline. My remains had been placed inside a black plastic bag.
The next morning, two prison guards brought my wife to identify
my body, which had been moved inland to a burial spot a bit further
from the shore. A shovel had been placed beside it. They opened the
body bag. She confirmed my identity and signed a paper verifying
that my death resulted from a betrayal of my country. An official took
a picture of my corpse and attached it to his file.

Left alone, she removed my remains from the bag. Then she dug
a shallow grave and searched the area for stones to place around
my body. She wept alone for a long time, rubbing her tears onto my
eyes so that we could mourn together. Just yesterday, we had been
embracing each other, dreaming of a bright future, anticipating a
reunion with all our children. Now she was heartbroken, suffering
in the living world while I watched over her, helpless. Eventually she
rolled up the bag and carefully placed it under my feet. My body
would decompose faster and be easier to exhume later. Then she
began shovelling sand over my body.

When we fell in love, my wife asked me if I would still love her
when she was no longer young and beautiful. She wondered if
Heaven would take both of us from the earth at the same time so
that we would always be together. Now I wished I could tell her the
answer to both questions.

"My dearest wife, my love for you is eternal. I loved you in life and
now also in death. I could not step through the Door of Heaven. I
want to be with you, to drift beside you as a ghost, to continue loving

you as a ghost. I would be lonely if I stayed in Heaven while you remained on this earth. My conscience torments me for leaving you to take care of our children on your own. I want to continue to carry out my responsibilities as best as I can. I will wait for you, forever, in life and in death.

"We will see each other again. I will wait for you as a ghost, and when you approach the Door of Heaven, I will be there to greet you. We will hold hands and enter together."

I met the young woman who would become my wife for the first time in 1954, when she boarded the bus to her hometown of Mũi Né. I was in my last year at the military school in Đà Lạt, taking advantage of a short leave to visit my mother in my hometown of Huế. While boarding the bus, the bus driver asked me to help with the passengers' luggage. Among them was a beautiful young woman wearing a nurse's uniform, who asked me politely to be careful while handling her luggage, since it contained fragile medical equipment.

I wanted to sit near her but the bus was full and I could only find a seat at the rear, a few rows behind her. For the entire trip, I could not help but watch her, even though I could only see the back of her head. I noticed she took her nursing hat off and tied her long ebony hair into a ponytail. I looked forward to finding out her name when I helped unload the luggage.

The bus slowly pulled to a stop to drop the passengers off at Phan Thiết station. I got off the bus quickly to prepare for unloading. She got off the bus and came to stand beside me. I heard her soft voice, "Could you please get my luggage first? I need to catch another bus to Mũi Né." This was my chance. My heart fluttered.

"May I know your name?"

No answer. She only smiled. I intentionally removed luggage for other passengers first, to prolong the moment she was beside me.

"Please, may I know your name?" I asked again. This time I stared a bit longer. Her smile was even more beautiful with the wind blowing loose strands of hair across her face. Still no answer.

I reluctantly handed the luggage to her. I was about to repeat my question when she turned and hurried toward the bus to Mũi Né. I thought about her smile for the remainder of my trip. Love began to unveil its wonders to me, one by one.

I planned to find her at the main hospital as soon as I returned to Đà Lạt. During a short weekend break, I put on my best clothes and ventured to the hospital. Entering the main building, I strolled around, hoping that I could spot her among the other nurses. When that failed, I approached the reception desk.

"May I help you?" asked a nurse who was sitting behind the counter.

"Yes. I am looking for a nurse."

"Are you sick or injured anywhere?"

"No, I am looking for an acquaintance, and I think she works as a nurse at this hospital."

"What's her name?"

I couldn't answer. All I knew was that she was from Mũi Né.

"Honestly, I don't know her name."

The nurse who asked me the question started to giggle. Other nurses walked over and joined her. They all looked at me, amused.

"I think I'll come back some other time." As I walked out of the hospital, the sound of their laughter followed me.

I sat on the bench outside, near the main gate, not wanting to leave just yet. I looked around, hoping to see her by chance. I sat and watched doctors and nurses walking by. I noticed patients and children, sick and injured, being carried through the emergency door and recognized for the first time the intensity of the daily responsibilities of health care workers, the compassion and courage necessary to soothe physical pain. I went back to my dorm, still thinking of her smile and planning to return.

The second time I visited the hospital, I was determined to find her, no matter how awkward I might look. The same nurse was behind the counter.

She recognized me but held in her giggles. "Are you still looking for your acquaintance? Do you know her name this time?"

"Honestly, I still don't know her name. But I know her hometown is Mũi Né."

"Why didn't you say that the last time? She is Nurse Võ. She works in the infant ward. Walk out the front door, turn to the right. A bit farther down you will see a sign that says infant ward."

I could not thank her enough and walked fast, arriving at the infant ward to find men and pregnant women walking in and out. When some new parents emerged with their baby, I caught a glimpse of a nurse holding an infant and recognized her, even from the back.

There were stone benches set outside for visitors; I sat on one and waited, oblivious to curious stares. Then, finally, she walked out, taking her break. I stood up. She smiled and I could see she knew who I was. Our eyes met and we remained wordless for a moment. The nametag attached to her uniform read Võ Thị Sĩ.

My heart pounded faster. "I could not forget your smile. I finally found you."

For months afterward, I skipped classes and borrowed my superior's jeep to pick her up after her shifts at the hospital. Eventually, she explained her reluctance to tell me her name.

"My first name and my siblings' first names were set in stone before we were even born. My parents planned to have four children and to give each child an auspicious first name in order: Sĩ (Intellectual), Khoa (Success), Phát (Prosperity), Tài (Affluence). It did not matter if the baby was a boy or a girl, he or she would have to take the name according to the prescribed order. I was the first born, so I had to take the name Sĩ. But it sounds more like a boy's name."

It had never occurred to me that I would get married. Nearly twenty-nine, I was already considered too old, and I was in military college, potentially destined for a combat zone. When, in July of 1954, the Geneva Conference divided Vietnam at the seventeenth parallel, the war with the French ended. After she finished her last year of nursing training, she accepted my proposal and, in 1955, became my beloved wife.

Thirty-one years to the day after that first bus ride, I left my wife alone on this earth. But my soul was with her and my sons all the time they were in prison. Because they were only fifteen and thirteen years old, Phổ and Phấn were allowed to remain with their mother. Children and most women were housed together in one large cell and were often left alone. Male prisoners were held in separate cells and interrogated to reveal the identities of the people who had organized the escape, but our captain and the boat owners had died. There were no trials; all prisoners were immediately condemned as guilty the moment they were captured.

Hungry and full of grief, my family suffered beyond what I can describe. Every day was a struggle to stay alive. The prisoners' diet consisted of small amounts of rice that, whether by accident or design, were occasionally mixed with chicken feces. Phổ, always so meticulous, was forced to live in filth. He had weighed less than four pounds at birth and had been nicknamed Cobbiert after the French-made calcium supplement he was given daily; now he was under-nourished again. Phấn, the most handsome and patient of all my children—his nickname Johnny meant a gracious gift from God—witnessed fellow prisoners fighting for sleeping places, water and food.

I followed every step they took. I wrapped myself around them every night as they slept. I tried to comfort them every time they cried. I felt the immense sorrow in their hearts and felt a corresponding pain in my own. I tried to hug them, but they did not respond. I was invisible to them. God had warned me—I was a miserable ghost, a helpless soul.

Young children and prisoners with severe illness were often released early because of the lack of available medical treatment or, perhaps, out of compassion. My wife was unwell, suffering from episodes of light hemorrhaging. After three months, my family was included in a group of prisoners being released from Côn Sơn Prison. They were transported back to the mainland and to their homes, where they would be covertly monitored by local communist officials. My wife, Phổ and Phấn would return to our house in Đà Lạt, now occupied by my first daughter, Mỹ Phương. Twenty-nine years old, she had chosen to remain behind in Vietnam with her husband and three young children. Her nickname, Hélène, means shining light; now she would need to be the shining light for her mother and brothers.

The day before they were to leave, the warden allowed my wife to visit my grave. She walked alone carrying a few sticks of incense, her steps slowing with the growing burden of her sorrow. A storm had passed through the island a few days earlier; my gravesite was littered with palm leaves and the wind had flattened the small hump of sand and stones that marked the spot. She collected more rocks and once again placed them on top of my grave to mark the location. Then she lit the incense, knelt beside the burial place and wept until nearly dusk. No prison guards were called to search for her. Where could she go?

My conscience tormented me—my wife was now alone, my death an abandonment. How would she handle the aftermath of this disaster? Despite my anguish, I reminded myself that the peace that would come from forever departing this world would have to wait. I longed for the time that my family could be reunited. I desperately wanted to protect my children and my wife, still separated on two different continents.

I wondered if my six other children in Canada had heard about our family's tragedy. The ritual mourning period of one hundred days was supposed to mark the end of tears. But I asked myself the same question over and over: Would the tears ever end for my family?

My first son, Phiên, was twenty-seven. We gave him the nickname of Paul, meaning humility, because of his kind and easygoing nature. His interest in music had influenced his younger siblings; since the day he begged his mother for a guitar, Phiên and my children had all surprised me with their musical ability. His wife, Thu Hà, twenty-five years old, was a perfect match for him. Her name means autumn breeze and aptly described her nature. How could Phiên and Thu Hà cope with two violent deaths?

My second daughter, Hằng Phương (Mélanie), was more practical. She loved to cook and, at twenty-five, had been in charge of the family meal for over ten years. Now we would never eat together again. I worried that even my second son, Phán (Bert), twenty-three and known for his sense of humour, wouldn't be able to comfort her. I deeply regretted the responsibilities I had asked Phú, my third son, to accept, unintentionally forcing him to become wise at a young age. He resembled me the most in terms of character and, at twenty, had already fulfilled the meaning of his nickname Bernard, signifying courage. Now my death and that of his sister would be added to his burden.

My wife had always worried that our third daughter, Diệu Phương, nicknamed Jolie, was—like her younger sister Lan Phương—sensitive, and the two had always been very close. How would Diệu

Phương, a gentle soul of nineteen, handle such immense loss? And what about my fourth son, Phi? He most closely resembled me physically and we gave him the nickname Robert, meaning brightness. Could his serene nature handle such a blow at just sixteen?

Grass started to grow on top of my grave, spreading to become a field, growing so tall that it hid and protected my burial site. I continued to search for Lan Phương's body near the spot where the boat sank. Under the waves of the Pacific Ocean, I found the wrecks of other boats and the scattered bones of other escapees. Their bodies occasionally washed ashore and were buried by the locals. I searched among them too, but to no avail. I wandered the isolated beaches of this island, listening to the roaring waves, a ceaseless rhythm that expressed the regret of mistakes that could not be undone and sorrow that could never be cured.

CHAPTER 2

June Sisters

Two light taps on the lenses of my glasses woke me up. I had fallen asleep on the sofa in the living room, and I was alone. Perhaps it was my imagination, fueled by the stress of preparing myself and my three daughters for our trip to Vietnam. As I sat up, I saw our six bags standing neatly by the front door, ready to depart with us the next morning, June 11, 2008. My children had been packing for two months prior to this trip. They had also been writing journals and doing research, excited to visit their mother's homeland. After twenty-five years, I felt both sentimental and overwhelmed.

Later that night, I dreamed of my father. He was wearing his familiar dark sunglasses and his neat white shirt. He didn't speak, but his reassuring smile, a constant of my childhood, said everything, binding my past and my future. I awoke to darkness, desperate to return to the bright light and vivid colours of the dream, to hold onto that precious moment forever.

Mother said she still felt his spirit, especially when she did not feel well, and maintained that he liked to visit my home. Once, when she was visiting my first house in Hamilton, she saw him standing by the bed as she took a nap. It seemed he desperately wanted to say something but couldn't get any words out. Anxious and fearful, Mother was suddenly determined to go home despite the ice storm that was keeping everyone inside. When I refused to take her, insisting it was too dangerous to drive, she called my oldest brother, Phiên. Warm-hearted to all of us, and especially to Mother, he braved the icy streets to take her home and put her mind at rest.

She told me she also saw Father in a dream after I moved to this house, but this time his spirit was not a sorrowful figure. Instead, he carried a ladder from the garage and fixed the leaking roof, the one I had never mentioned to anyone. When she woke up, she asked me if my house had a leak in the family room. I was stunned.

Mother maintained that Father's spirit lived in my house, surrounding me, taking care of me. The stubborn, sceptical part of my mind naturally created doubts, but I fought them off, willing myself to believe her. I wanted so badly to prove his existence. It was not my imagination—his smile was always real, delicately engraved in my memory. Now, as I prepared to return to Vietnam, I asked myself the question I had asked so many times before: Would this trip help me fully accept the reality of his death? And that of my beloved sister?

My sister, Lan Phương, and I were both born in June, ten years apart, during the monsoon season. Many people, especially those of previous generations, consider rain the tears of Heaven and I often wonder if our fate as sisters was foreshadowed by the month of our birth.

A thick fog covered the ground as my mother entered labour early on the morning of June 15, 1976. This baby would be the tenth child, and my mother was sure it was a girl. She openly told us that this pregnancy was unexpected; she had not wanted to bear a child in this time of political instability. After the end of the lengthy war, the country was transitioning from democracy to a communist regime, and life was full of uncertainty.

We watched Father take Mother to the hospital on the bicycle. For her other deliveries, he had driven her in his green Jeep Cherokee, but this baby would be born into a different world. The night before, I heard Mother tell Father, "This child will not know anything about our family car. She also will never know the taste of Enfalac or SMA."

Father tried to comfort her. "I will go to Mũi Né to get your mother." I knew he was trying to hide his own disappointment and helplessness.

The rain came around noon. Father returned home from the hospital, soaking wet despite his thick raincoat. We surrounded him, all talking at once. "Father, Father, how is Mother? When can we see the baby?"

"Your mother is fine. She was crying while in labour, but as soon as your sister was born, she smiled. She is resting with the baby right now and will be home in a few days." I could see how tired Father was, but he still tried to be cheerful. "Tomorrow, I will go to Mũi Né. Grandmother will stay with us for a while to help take care of the baby."

The raincoat fell twice as he tried to hang it up, a consequence of losing the sight in one eye before I was born. He always wore dark sunglasses when outside and lighter glasses inside. Growing up, I once covered one of my eyes and tried to move around. I had to turn wide angles to avoid bumping into the sharp corner of the table and grabbed onto things to avoid losing my balance or tripping.

My parents named all their daughters with the first name Phương, which means virtue and visionary. We were given different middle names and were generally addressed by both. Father said our names were tied to the personalities and virtues he envisioned in each of us: Mỹ Phương means extraordinary beauty, Hằng Phương relates to the soft beauty of the moon, and my name, Diệu Phương, means gentleness. The baby's middle name would be Lan, a rare orchid that thrives in the climate of our town, Đà Lạt. Lan Phương was like a white orchid, a combination of innocence, purity, elegance and beauty.

My mother's younger brother, Uncle Khoa, once commented to Mother about my middle name. He said Diệu was meant to be a first name and should not be used as a middle name. "Diệu is used in Buddhist names as a special middle name for Buddhist nuns. For an ordinary woman, having this middle name means bearing a heavy burden in life, forever seeking harmony and peace that may not come until her old age. The name predicts her future."

Mother replied, "But we gave her the nickname of Jolie when we noticed her brightness as a baby. Whenever we cradled her in our arms, she immediately gave us the prettiest smile. I am sure it will balance out the meaning of her middle name."

Grandmother came for six months to help Mother take care of Lan Phương. Whenever she cried, Grandmother said, "She was born in June. Babies born in June cry more than other babies and are predicted to have a hard life." With twenty-four grandchildren, I thought perhaps Grandmother had forgotten that I was born in June as well.

As Mother had predicted, Lan Phương grew up drinking mostly broth made from rice. Once in a while, Father brought home a can of condensed milk he obtained from the black market that we diluted with boiled water.

Each of us had our own duties and we took turns helping with Lan Phương, but I spent all my free time with my Grandmother, who taught me how to care for a baby. After six months, Grandmother left to go back to Mũi Né, a fishing town in the southern part of the country, by the warm part of the Pacific Ocean. She was sad to go but the cold and damp weather of the plateau hurt her knees. Before she left, Grandmother told me, "Jolie, I have trained you well. You are the primary caregiver for Lan Phương from now on."

Shortly after Grandmother left, a strange incident occurred. As usual, Lan Phương had gone to sleep between Hằng Phương and me. However, in the morning we found her sleeping peacefully on the cold cement floor, on top of the edge of the mosquito netting. We were horrified but puzzled—she still could not crawl but had somehow slipped off the bed and landed on the cement without hurting herself and without making a sound. When Grandmother visited us a few years later, I told her of this incident. She asked me to repeat the details and then confirmed them with Hằng Phương. Grandmother was apprehensive and finally had a serious private conversation with Mother and Father. She was convinced this was *độn thổ*, a hint from Heaven that foretold my sister was destined to die young.

We two sisters, Lan Phương and Diệu Phương, although ten years apart, were inseparable. We played with each other and read each other bedtime stories. We went to school together and did homework together. We could not be parted. Lan Phương never wanted to be out of my sight and cried if I was not near her. Each week, when Phú and I lined up to buy rice with our food stamps, we would take turns piggybacking Lan Phương.

When Lan Phương was very young, Phú was the only one who could convince her to let me leave for school. Later, after he had left for Saigon, and I was in high school, no one in the family could persuade her so she came to school with me, happy to be with older kids my age. My teacher allowed Lan Phương to sit near me or to wait in the corner; she was quiet and content as long as she could see me. On Lan Phương's first day of school, she cried, throwing a tantrum, insisting I stay with her. Her teacher gave in and asked me to stay that day, so I became a Grade 1 student again, learning everything I already knew.

As Lan Phương grew older, we took turns reading each other bedtime stories. One of our favourites was Hans Christian Andersen's *The Little Mermaid*. On the nights we did not want to read, we made up stories for each other. Then we turned our stories into a play we acted out on our main playground, the temple compound near our home. One of the main characters was a mermaid. We believed that mermaids existed and wished for a chance to travel by boat on the vast ocean so that we could see one. In quieter moments, we sat under the statue of Phật Bà Quan Âm, the Bodhisattva of Compassion. We prayed for peace, for being together forever, for death to never come into our world.

Almost every evening, I played the guitar while Lan Phương sang. Sometimes she sang songs I taught her, but we especially enjoyed making up our own. One of our favourites was "When the Last Leaf Falls." On a cold and rainy night, Death comes to a poor, wretched house and knocks on the door, ready to collect the soul of a young girl dying of an incurable illness. But Death is touched by the mother's anguish and, pointing to three leaves on an old tree, promises to return when the final leaf falls. We added music and performed the song for Father.

WHEN THE LAST LEAF FALLS.

Raindrops or teardrops?
For forlorn tree or wretched soul?
Raindrops fall upon the leaves.
One by one, each leaf drifts down.
The last raindrop falls on the last leaf,
The last to float to the ground,
As the fierce wind hounds.
Death comes again to collect the tiny soul.
The bereft mother sheds her last tear.

"I remember every single word, Father." Lan Phương was proud of her memorizing skill. "Do you want to hear us sing again?"

"Yes, I love hearing my daughters sing, but this sad song?" Father hesitated.

While Lan Phương sang enthusiastically, I could tell Father wanted to ask me if I had taught her anything more cheerful. He finally found an opportunity to ask me about it when he took me to the tailor for a shirt.

By 1982, the communist government was easing restrictions, the black market was slowly diminishing, and many merchants were finally reopening their stores. Father took me to see my Aunt Hiền who had a fabric shop at Chợ Đà Lạt, the main shopping centre in the city.

Aunt Hiền greeted us with enthusiasm. "Your daughter has such fair skin tones. Red or pink will be good colours for her."

"I don't like red or pink. Those colours are too bright. Red is the colour of blood!" I whispered to Father, but Aunt Hiền heard what I said.

"Most girls like pink. How old are you? Sixteen? Girls of your age should wear bright colours. Red is not necessarily for blood. It also means victory!" She picked up both the bright pink and red pieces of fabric and tried to wrap them around my shoulders.

Father reminded his sister, "Let her choose. Jolie, take your time and pick what you like."

I finally chose a white fabric with a pattern of tiny mushrooms coloured with both red and pink.

Father then took me to a nearby tailor shop. While waiting for my turn to be measured, Father said, "Jolie, tell me more about that song Lan Phương sang, 'When the Last Leaf Falls.'"

I recited the verses in Vietnamese.

Hạt mưa rơi hay giọt lệ rơi?
Mưa rơi trên cây tàn úa.
Có phải Trời đang khóc thương
cho những linh hồn khổ hạnh?

Khi chiếc lá cuối cùng rơi.
Là khi Thần Chết lại đến.
Là giọt lệ cuối cùng.
Đọng trên đôi mắt Mẹ.

Father voice was sad as he asked, "Why do you use the words 'forlorn tree'?"

"Because the storm will bring the old tree down."

"And you're comparing raindrops to the tears of Heaven?"

"Yes, Father, I wanted to express that Heaven cries when the human has no tears left. The guitar chords are easy too. I just switch between chords D, B minor, A7, G, and E minor."

"The last sentence hints that when Death arrived, Death also collected the mother's soul."

"Yes, Father. She shed her last tears. She never cried again because she died."

"Jolie, you are aware that your mother and I lost your older brother, Phu, when he was almost two years old. He was such a handsome and smart little boy."

I had often looked at Phu's framed image on the altar and wondered about his death. I wondered what it would have been like to have another handsome older brother.

"Father, how did he die?"

"He was sick with a fever. All the children were sick, it seemed like a normal illness. But with Phu, it was strange. The night before, I stayed up and cradled him the entire night. His fever went down. I had to go to work the next day and his fever came back, but your mother knew what to do and kept him cool. She told me he kept sitting up, looking out the window to watch for me, listening for the sound of my jeep. When I got home, we took him to see the doctor at the clinic. But his fever got worse and he died the same evening. Your mother said it seemed like he knew." Father's sunglasses hid his tears but I could hear them in his voice.

"We also lost your younger sister, Hồng Phương, when she was only three months old. She died from a combination of high fever and diarrhea. She was as bright as you."

I was sorry that I had made Father recall such sad memories. Seeing my expression, he tried to put on his usual warm smile but I noticed it was only lukewarm today. "Your mother and I grieve the deaths of Phu and Hồng Phương, but we have trained our minds to bury the anguish deep inside our hearts, so that we can move on with our life."

The lady tailor came to our seats, and our conversation shifted to what style I wanted for this special shirt. I followed her to the measuring room. Discreetly looking back, I saw Father use his handkerchief to wipe the tears from his eyes. He then stood up and lit his cigarette.

On the way home, Father said, "Jolie, your middle name, Diệu, has another meaning beside gentleness, and far from what your Uncle Khoa explained to your mother."

He had my attention.

"Diệu is part of the descriptive words Kì Diệu, hidden talent. Your two names together mean vision and dream. Life is a struggle sometimes, but you need to discover your strength, your talent, then search hard for your dreams and follow your passion in the midst of chaos."

Sensing my confusion. Father paused, then continued. "If you face difficulties in life, be strong, always try your best. The most important point is to live your life with kindness to others and to yourself. Then good things will come to you."

CHAPTER 3

THE TIGER

Tigers are considered the king of the forest in Vietnamese culture. I was born in the year of the tiger and my mother always said that I also bore its "full and powerful spirit." She believed I was compatible with the mountains and that my ambitions would be realized in this environment.

In 1961 I left my hometown of Huế and brought my wife and our three children to Quảng Đức, a mountain town surrounded by thick, untouched forests that were home to tigers, monkeys and other wildlife. We had lived in Huế for the previous six years, building our first home on a piece of land my father gave us. My wife worked as an on-call nurse and cared for our family. When the Indochina war ended, I had remained in military college but switched my focus to architecture, and Quảng Đức was rumoured to be an area of opportunity. Its vast timber resources made it prosperous, and its geography made it strategically important, especially now that hostility was intensifying between North and South Vietnam and the growing presence of Americans was deepening political unrest. My older brother, Kha, and his family accompanied us and together we started a construction business, getting contracts from the Americans to build roads, schools, a hospital, houses and military barracks.

As our new business grew, so did my family, and my wife and I celebrated the arrival of more sons. But around us the war was escalating. North Vietnamese soldiers, also known as Viet Cong, built underground bases along the edge of the nearby Buôn Ới River that became targets for South Vietnamese forces. Our first home was destroyed during a bombardment in 1962. I was away on a business trip to Saigon and came home to a pile of ashes. No words could describe how horrified I felt until I discovered that my family had been saved by my wife's quick thinking. When the house was hit, she had poured water on the mattress and put all four children on it. Then she covered them with wet blankets and pulled them out of the burning house. She told me she had been prepared for disaster because the owls that gathered on our roof at night were a bad omen.

I built another house next to my brother's, by the river. Both houses were connected to an underground cave where we retreated whenever we were awakened by bombing or gunfire. My brother would scold his children to behave and to stay quiet while my wife sang lullabies to ours. I put on a brave face and guarded the door.

The business was thriving but was counter-balanced with tragedy; due to the lack of a modern hospital and rare medicines, we lost a son in 1963 and an infant daughter in 1967. I also contracted an eye disease and lost the vision in my right eye. I often wondered what would have happened if we had lived in a bigger city, such as Saigon. Would my eye have been cured? Would my son and my daughter have survived their illnesses?

My wife was licensed to sell medicines so I built and opened a pharmacy for her to operate. I employed many villagers, and many of them were also her patients. They often paid her with eggs, chickens and rice; one time, she was paid with a pet monkey trained to do light household chores. My wife worried about its unpredictable behaviour around our young children, so when it imitated her and began chopping vegetables using the kitchen knife, she was horrified and suggested that I release it back to the forest. I drove it to the edge of the forest and let it go, but it found its way back the same day. The second time, I covered its eyes and drove my jeep further into the forest. This time, the pet monkey seemed to understand that it was not welcome in our home—it jumped out of the jeep, made a strange sound and disappeared into the thick woods. As I watched it go, I stood beside the jeep and lit a cigarette. I breathed in the nicotine and breathed out the smoke, letting my thoughts flow with it, carried on the wind into the mountains. In this rare moment of solitude, I thought of my mother explaining that, because I was both conceived and born in the year of the tiger, I was a potent "full tiger." I had been successful in this land. I was just turning forty and was already a millionaire.

However, those nights when we sheltered in the underground cave, I often had conflicted feelings about what I was trying to achieve. Among my collection of cars, there was a Rolls Royce, several Dodge pick-up trucks, a Jeep Cherokee with three rows of bench seats and a Chevrolet van. I often drove my children to visit construction sites in my favourite French-made automobile: a black Citroen Traction Avant. But those same children were experiencing the direct effects of war, their sleep constantly disturbed.

I taught all my children to grow fruit and vegetables from the seeds that I brought back from my business trips and we raised pigs for meat. On less busy days, I would take Phiên to the river to fish. During hard times, times of intense bombing when American soldiers closed roads, school, and supermarkets and the whole town was under curfew, we harvested the fruit and lived off the vegetable garden, our pigs and fish.

One day I arrived home from a long business trip to find my children distraught, my wife angry and the whole garden destroyed. The children were tired of the monkeys stealing the bananas from the trees, so Phiên had decided to discourage them by sprinkling the bananas with red chili powder. The children laughed with excitement as they hid inside the house, waiting for the monkeys to enter the trap. Sure enough, the monkeys arrived and feasted on the spicy bananas. Then they screamed and jumped up and down wildly, running and wrecking everything around them. Some lay down, holding their mouths and tummies and crying at the same time. Some licked the dirt, desperate to ease the pain on their tongues. The children's excitement turned into a scary feeling as the monkeys left. Shortly after, they returned with the entire troop of angry monkeys, who wrecked the garden in an act of revenge.

I explained to my children that monkeys used to dominate these western stretches of Vietnam. Their habitat had been invaded and, like us, they were suffering in this war-infested land. I had come to realize that the Americans could build roads, houses and fully developed villages, but they could just as easily destroy them. Just like the monkeys, our benefactors could turn on us at any time.

The Americans paid me in cash. After each deal was signed, I would come home with a briefcase full of money. My young son, Phú, would run out to greet me and carry the briefcase inside. Sometimes, it weighed as much as he did and he would have to drag it along the floor. There was no bank where we could make deposits, so my wife sewed long, thin fabric tubes to store the American bills. We hid the tubes within the walls. Whenever I travelled to Saigon on business, she would tie them around my waist, hidden under my thick clothes. I used the money to buy gold that I brought home to again be hidden within the walls of the house.

The fighting continued to escalate. The constant hiding in the family cave, fearing our homes would be bombed, was taking a toll, and almost every day we heard of new lives lost. My brother became increasingly fearful. When he lost his oldest son in a motorcycle accident, the stress overwhelmed him and he lost interest in operating the business with me. He abandoned the business and his house and moved his family to the relative safety of Đà Lạt. I reminded myself that living on this mountain was only temporary, that once I had enough money to keep my family safe in either the best or worst circumstances, we would also leave.

Driving home from inspecting a construction site one night, I discovered that the main road was closed—a Viet Cong soldier has been spotted earlier in the day and the South Vietnamese soldiers were searching for him. Scheduling delays had held me up and I was anxious to get home so, the moon being full, I decided to take the dirt road along the edge of the forest, near the river. When my jeep overheated on the bridge over a shallow creek, I opened the hood, then took buckets down to the creek for water. As I was returning, I saw a huge tiger move along the dirt road and hop on top of the vehicle. I was not altogether surprised. Land mines and chemical bombs had destroyed the richness of the mountain habitat; many villagers had been killed by tigers coming out of the deep woods to drink from creeks that were now traversed by bridges.

Our eyes locked. The animal just sat and stared at me. I threw the buckets and water splashed on both the animal and the hot engine, the clanking sound breaking the eerie silence. The tiger jumped off the roof, in the process hitting the hood with enough force to close it. I jumped into the jeep, shut the door, started the engine and floored the gas pedal. I heard the tiger roar behind me and closed my eyes for a moment as a chill ran down my spine. I prayed to the Bodhisattva of Compassion to bring me home safely to my children as, through the mirrors, I watched the huge animal give chase. Finally, it decided to stop pursuing its prey and receded into the distance.

That evening, I was shaken. My wife was horrified, and my children screamed, but with time my adventure became a story often told at bedtime. The children laughed when I told them I could have won a medal for auto racing, but the experience shaped my thoughts about fate. I had survived confrontations with the king of the mountain and the chaos of war; my fate was to die in the waters of the Pacific Ocean.

The night I met the tiger, my wife also faced a dangerous situation. She was making dinner with the back door open so that she could add any scraps to the pot on the stone stove outside, the one we used to feed the pigs. A man wearing a dirty black shirt and pants, his face hidden under a straw hat and a black scarf, suddenly appeared, asking for food. As she ran into the living room, urging the children to hide, the stranger grabbed the pigs' food and ate right from the pot. Then he left.

When the soldiers arrived, my wife said nothing about her visitor, and the children, as instructed, stayed quiet. But he was caught and shot anyway, buried in a shallow grave that was later dug up by wild animals. He was a Viet Cong, but he was also my fellow countryman, driven from his cave by hunger. A Vietnamese whose last meal was pig food.

Money was made but could also be lost. After the main routes to Saigon were closed due to land mines, I hired military planes to bring in trucks filled with the building materials I needed to fulfill my contracts. On one flight, the plane experienced a malfunction but was too heavy to land safely. To save lives, the pilot opened the back of the plane and dumped all the trucks into the ocean. I lost all the materials and one of my most profitable contracts. My wife and I both knew we needed to leave. We planned to return to Đà Lạt, the city where we met. It was both a practical and a romantic choice, and one ultimately delayed by events beyond our control.

During the Lunar New Year celebration in 1968, North Vietnamese forces launched a series of surprise attacks in various cities throughout South Vietnam. The Tết Offensive, as it was known, turned out to be a disastrous military failure but its consequences for the civilians of South Vietnam were also severe. The South Vietnamese government was outraged by the success with which Viet Cong guerrillas had infiltrated villages and businesses. During the day, these guerrillas were ordinary civilians with legitimate jobs; at night they operated as Viet Cong. In response, the South Vietnamese government launched an aggressive campaign to find and eliminate these groups. Many honest and upright citizens were unjustly arrested, imprisoned and interrogated to reveal names of their alleged co-conspirators. In October of 1968, I became one of them.

The South Vietnamese policemen stopped my jeep while I was passing through a checkpoint and took me to the Gia Nghĩa police station for questioning. Sensing that I would be detained through the night, I paid a soldier to drive my jeep home and send word to my wife, who was pregnant. I was relieved my family would be spared the shock of seeing me apprehended at our home.

The policemen told me I was suspected of aiding the Viet Cong. Many villagers and their relatives had moved to Quảng Đức to be employed by my company, but it never occurred to me that I employed Viet Cong guerrillas or spies. Now I was told that some of them had been convicted as undercover agents. As a respected businessman, the policemen treated me with caution, and I was treated properly throughout the interrogation. They decided to send me to Quân Lao, the military prison located in Nha Trang, for further investigation and to await trial. Prisoners held in military prison were treated more humanely than those sent to civilian facilities.

I stayed in the military prison for one year. On the Lunar New Year of 1969, I was allowed a visit from my wife. I felt sad, happy and helpless seeing her with her pregnant belly. Sitting across from each other, neither of us could speak at first. I didn't want to say a lot, I only wanted to hear her voice. I knew the time that we were allowed was short but minutes of silence passed until I asked her how she was feeling and how the children were.

"I am feeling fine. I feel relieved seeing you healthy. Did they give you a hard time?"

"No. They treat me okay. Anything bad, I can handle it."

My wife lowered her voice. "Some villagers and employees went to the police station to complain, declaring that you are innocent. They demanded the police release you."

"The villagers and my employees are very honest and work hard for their living. I don't think and never thought there are Viet Cong guerrillas among them." I shook my head.

"If there were Viet Cong guerrillas among the workers, there is no way that we could know."

My wife had brought home cooking for me. Now she paused and picked up chopsticks to put a piece of grilled beef onto my rice bowl. "You always took good care of the workers. They took a risk, showing up at the police station to voice their opinions. Some of them have had to leave town to look for work elsewhere. A few of them said they would not be able to find better wages."

I ate the homemade food in silence. "Tell me about the children."

She told me that Mỹ Phương, Phiên and Hằng Phương were staying with her younger brother Khoa in a rented home at Đà Lạt. He was studying at the military college, the same one I attended. The younger ones were still with her.

My wife was very intelligent, a practical woman and a problem solver. I worried that she would try to do too much. "I think you should take the children and go to Đà Lạt until you gave birth. Don't try to visit me often. The trip from Đà Lạt to Nha Trang or from Quảng Đức to here is hard on you. I will be fine. Take good care of yourself."

"I will arrange to give birth to this baby at Đà Lạt. I have been praying at the temple whenever I have time. Please, take good care of yourself and come home safe."

"I know it is just a matter of time before they release me. There is no evidence to support their allegation."

A heavy silence descended upon us. We understood each other's thoughts. Sometimes all we could do was pray for the resolution of factors that we could not control.

"In this bag, there are the English books that you asked for. Also, I packed some medications for you. And in this package, I packed a few cartons of your favourite Craven A cigarettes."

I spent my free time studying English. The warden allowed me to walk to the beach twice a week where I collected scrap materials —wood, metal, cardboard, whatever I could find—to build an architectural model, a peaceful Vietnamese town shaped like an S, mirroring the unique shape of Vietnam. The warden provided me with essential tools and blocked off a corner on the exercise yard where I constructed a model city completed with a modern hospital, schools, a movie theatre, parks with playgrounds, a tower for clean water, a temple, a church, a museum, a public library and houses built like villas. After I completed it, the warden told me I had forgotten to build a penitentiary—the model was proof of my dream, but far from the reality of my efforts in Quảng Đức, a beautiful town blessed with vast resources but plagued by war. Despite all our efforts, the conflict ruined everything, stripping bare the beauty of nature to reveal the ugliness of humanity at its worst.

After a lengthy investigation, and after finding no evidence to support their accusations, the policemen put me in front of the military court and declared me innocent. I was released and went to Đà Lạt to greet my five-month-old son, Phi, the only one of my children whose birth I was not able to attend.

It took me more than a year to resolve my business. Mỹ Phương, Phiên and Hằng Phương were settled in Đà Lạt; the rest of us made frequent trips between there and Quảng Đức, gradually transferring what possessions we could. On each trip, my wife pretended to be pregnant so that we could hide all the gold around her fake-pregnant tummy. Gold ingots were also sewn inside the lining of our coats and hidden in secret compartments of our carry-on bags. Whatever couldn't be moved was cheaply sold or given away. Finally, I said a sad farewell to the villagers and my remaining employees and hired a military plane to leave Quảng Đức with my wife and my four younger children: Phán, Phú, Diệu Phương and baby Phi. The cargo also contained my green Jeep Cherokee.

CHAPTER 4

A BOWL OF SOUP

As the plane descended into Tân Sơn Nhất airport, toward the humidity and sweat of Saigon, I peered through the window hoping to identify a particular spot, an intersection beside a shattered brick wall where, twenty-five years ago, my father stood beside his bicycle, secretly waving a final farewell to my brothers, my sister and me. As our bus departed, dust from the tires blurred his smile and covered his dark sunglasses. What was the name of the street? What bus stop was that? I desperately wanted to remember everything about that moment. I should have paid more attention. I should have sealed it in my memory.

The dust, the noise and the heat woke me from my nap.

"Jolie, we are in Saigon. Hold tight to your bag even after you put it across your shoulder. There are lots of thieves around," Father reminded me. I picked up my blue Puma bag and turned to follow him as we left the bus station.

We took a cycle rickshaw to Bến Thành market where he bought me two sets of clothes and a small butterfly knife. I was the only one in the family who had not been to Saigon and I was overwhelmed by the fast pace and constant noise. It was a relief to enter the relative calm of a restaurant.

Father ordered three bowls of phở and my favourite sweet and salty lime drink, *Chanh Muối*. Once we were served, he waved to a dirty little boy panhandling outside the restaurant, signalling him to come in. He was half-Vietnamese, half-American, an abandoned child and a reminder of a brutal war. He ate the soup as fast as he could, alert to the possibility that someone could take the precious food away from him. I could not stop watching him and Father had to remind me to concentrate on finishing my own meal. He took the egg from his bowl and gently placed it into mine and I was suddenly aware of how loved and sheltered I was.

After we finished eating, we remained at the table while Father taught me how to operate the butterfly knife, using the strength of my wrist and applying the correct movement to flick the blade open. Then how to flick the blade back inside the handle and secure it with the spring latch.

"Jolie, you use this knife to protect yourself," he said, his tone serious.

I said nothing, not fully understanding what he meant.

"You will know if it ever happens. If you ever encountered danger, stay calm. The calmness will help you think wisely. Keep this knife hidden where you can grab it instantly."

I practised opening and closing the blade until Father gave me an approving nod. While I finished my drink, Father stepped outside to light a cigarette. He stood with his back against the wall, one hand in his pants pocket, the other moving the cigarette away from his mouth as he blew out thick white smoke. He lifted his head slightly to look at the sky through his dark sunglasses and I knew he was in his thinking mood.

After he finished his thinking-smoke, he took a seat facing me; I could sense that he was about to say something important. He looked serious, like he was trying to find the best words to explain. After a brief pause, he said, "Jolie, listen to me. Take my words seriously. I know your brothers would try to protect you if you ever encountered danger. However, there will be a time that you may not have me or your brothers around to protect you. Be aggressive when it comes to defending yourself, you are not doing anything wrong. If any men show bad intentions or try to hurt you, quickly use that knife, hold it firmly. If you can, aim it and slash the part in between their legs."

I was at a complete loss for words.

Father became even more serious. "Men with bad intentions who try to hurt women and innocent girls are living devils hiding in human form. They deserve to be treated with such measures. Just think of it as the best strategy, the best chance to defend yourself. You do nothing wrong by thinking or planning to take such extreme action. Those depraved devils deserve it."

I still could not fully imagine the dangerous situation I might have to confront. I wanted to ask questions but was interrupted by people walking into the restaurant for their evening meal. The waiter came to clean our table, encouraging us to make way for waiting customers. The panhandler boy returned and stood beside us; Father put his hands on the boy's shoulder and handed him some cash.

Father gave me a half-smile but said nothing more as we both stood and left the restaurant. As soon as we stepped outside, we were surrounded by men who asked us where we wanted to go, instantly offering a lower price than the initial bid. From the passenger seat of a cycle rickshaw (*xích lô*), I watched people maneuver around each other while riding on motorcycles, bicycles and three-wheeled trucks called Lambros (*xe lam*). The crowds, the noise and the smell of sewage wafting on the evening breeze made me dizzy. As we made our way to the hotel, I held on tight to my blue Puma bag, thinking of the butterfly knife inside.

That was the last day that I ever spent with my father, just the two of us.

CHAPTER 5

WAR

Đà Lạt is a plateau located about 200 kilometres south of Quảng Đức. The city is the largest in the central highland region of Vietnam and is situated 1,500 metres above sea level. During the 1890s, when Vietnam was a French colony, Alexandre Yersin, a French–Swiss bacteriologist and protégé of the renowned French chemist Lois Pasteur, popularized the plateau, which would become home to an important biological research centre named after his mentor. The French bequeathed architectural structures with Swiss and European charm that included villas, golf courses, a prestigious private boarding school, a modern hospital and the man-made Xuân Hương Lake surrounded by beautiful boulevards.

The weather in Đà Lạt is both changeable and consistent. Fog covers the ground in the morning, then turns into tiny droplets of water hugging the grass and trying to cling to the needles of the pine trees. The dews sparkles, reflecting magical hues under the bright sunlight. The rain comes in the afternoon, partially flooding the streets, the water flowing down the slope. People wear long raincoats while riding their motorcycles, swiftly maneuvering through the puddles and streams as part of their daily life. Then the rain stops, allowing the sun to shine through thick clouds to shape a rainbow that disperses its seven colours across the land. Near evening, the sunset melts away the greyish clouds, turning them into orangish and purplish patches on the sky.

Our life was peaceful on this plateau and the years from 1971 to 1975 were the best of our lives. I bought a house near Linh Sơn Temple and settled my family into a privileged life. Mỹ Phương and Hằng Phương went to Bùi Thị Xuân girls' school; Phiên and Phán attended the boys' school Trần Hưng Đạo, both the best available. They were all old enough to ride their bicycles to school. Phú and Diệu Phương were too young for these schools, so I enrolled them in the French private school Hùng Vương, formerly the prestigious Lycée Yersin, built in 1927 to educate the children of the French colonists. A man in the neighbourhood used his van to drive them to and from the school along with other local children, a thirty-minute trip. My fourth son, Phi, was still at home with his own nanny.

We added two more sons, Phổ and Phấn, and our extended family also grew. My two younger sisters and their families moved away from our hometown of Huế, building their lives in Đà Lạt near me and our older brother. I often arranged family vacations and took my children, nieces and nephews back to Huế to visit my mother, who lived with my younger brother, Trọng Châu, and his family. We celebrated every Lunar New Year in harmony, hearing the temple bell echoing for three consecutive days.

I opened a pharmacy for my wife to operate in Trại Mát, a small village that reminded us of Quảng Đức, located about seven kilometres from Đà Lạt. My wife continued to practise as a nurse, seeing patients at the pharmacy. I purchased a small farm close to the pharmacy and often took business trips to buy medications for our store, but I retired from construction and now had more free time for my children, the source of my energy and passion.

My ten living children were my true wealth, and I took them to the temple frequently, wanting them to appreciate a simple, peaceful life that respected the living and the dead. The temple, so near our home, became like a playground. The children often visited the tortoises

35

raised by the monks, their shells engraved with Buddhist characters representing harmony and peace.

Two years after I left Quảng Đức, I returned to exhume the bodies of my two dead children so that they could be buried in Mã Thánh cemetery, only a few kilometres from our home. It was evening when I returned home, too late to take their remains, sealed in clay pots inside a black suitcase, to the temple. As it was a bad omen to allow a dead body into a home—there is a strong traditional belief that the dead would pull the living into their world—I had to leave the suitcase outside overnight. I didn't explain, but when I asked my children not to touch it, I think they guessed what I was doing. They understood the dead had to be respected and needed to be near their living relatives.

Our idyllic existence ended when war finally arrived in Đà Lạt on an unusually hot day at the beginning of April 1975. The sky was very clear, and the many helicopters hovering over the soccer field near Xuân Hương Lake were clearly visible. South Vietnamese soldiers were deployed to protect the city.

Schools had closed early and I waited anxiously for Phú and Diệu Phương to return home to the rest of the family. When they didn't arrive, I walked to the driver's house to find out what had happened. He told me that he had driven to the school but couldn't wait for my children because the South Vietnamese soldiers were closing the streets. He'd had to leave before he became trapped with the other children, who had already made it to his van. I could not control my anger but, as the driver retreated into his house, I tried to calm myself, to figure out a way to find Phú and Diệu Phương.

I drove my Jeep Cherokee to school, hoping the children would have hidden nearby to wait for me. But I could not get past the military and the barricades. Armed soldiers ordered me to go home and warned me not to drive around the city. I returned to our house and traded my jeep for my bicycle, telling Phiên to go out on his bicycle to look for them as well. We circled the streets that remained open, among crowds of people frantically rushing home or looking for their children.

This peaceful city was suddenly facing the reality of war and residents were not prepared. That day, the merchants in the main shopping centre Chợ Đà Lạt closed up and were forced to leave; it would be years before they re-opened. Store owners in the city centre district, Khu Hoà Bình, shut their doors tightly. South Vietnamese soldiers guarded the streets to prevent looting and told people to leave the centre of the city; people who lived on the outskirts remained in their homes. As the communist soldiers were advancing, some people had already abandoned Đà Lạt and moved to Saigon, which was still controlled by the South Vietnamese government. Many others would soon follow.

I circled the open streets, desperately hoping to find my two children, until I was stopped by soldiers, who told me that I had to leave this central part of the city. When I arrived back at our house, I discovered that Phiên had found Phú and Diệu Phương walking home, thirsty and hungry. They told me that they had been unable to get to the van before it had to leave and had waited at the school, along with two friends, for a long time. Their friends' father finally arrived on a Vespa and advised my children to head home. They had run and walked, crossing the soccer field with helicopters hovering above them and hiding in the bushes, until they reached the centre of the city where they caught sight of their brother walking his bicycle.

That evening, while I washed their dirty feet, I tried to think of a way to keep my family safe. My wife and I made a crucial decision— we would pack some important belongings and the children into the jeep and leave the city, intending to take refuge at a Buddhist temple named Trùng Khánh near the town of Phan Rang. My wife had heard and believed that the North Vietnamese soldiers would not attack the temple and that staying with her uncle, who was the chief monk, would be safe.

It turned out that the normally three-hour drive to Phan Rang was a very slow one. We left before dawn and did not get to the temple before the sky was dark again. The mountain passes down from the plateau were full of people trying to flee the city on foot. Desperate men and women with young children filled the roads, along with slow-moving cars and trucks, ours included. The valley echoed with the crying of tired children and the frustrated voices of men and women.

Some men swore and threatened to smash my jeep. Some women placed their belongings and their children on the hood. Some men even hopped onto the rear bumper. I struggled for composure as I drove slowly among the weary, walking crowds, encouraging my frightened children to close their eyes and try to sleep, listening to Diệu Phương cry while her mother quietly scolded her.

At dawn the following day, we finally reached the end of the pass and approached the bridge that connected the highway to Phan Rang. Congestion eased as people scattered into fields, doing their best to ignore the dead bodies scattered there. Abandoned belongings were everywhere.

The bridge had been damaged by bombing so I decided to drive through the creek, which was stony and fairly shallow. I told my children to raise their feet to keep them dry. Diệu Phương cried louder, adding to everyone's frustration. We were all scared and hungry.

My jeep slowly moved through the creek and climbed onto the paved highway. I asked Phiên and Phán to open the side door to drain the water and we finally had a smooth drive—Diệu Phương stopped crying and everyone fell asleep for the remainder of the trip.

I kept on driving past the living and the dead, praying we would not be caught in a gunfight between soldiers of the North and those of the South.

I finally turned onto the road leading to the temple, more than a kilometre long and lined on both sides with beautiful palm trees. Whenever I had brought the children here for summer vacations, I loved driving slowly along this road. The wind brought the rich smell of full rice fields waiting to be harvested, and the sound of the palm leaves rustling against each other gave me a sense of peace. The same feeling now eased my fatigue.

I drove to the gate of the temple and received a warm welcome from my wife's uncle, the chief monk, who arranged for us to stay in three rooms in the temple's guest quarters. We were served vegan meals and then settled our children into their rooms. While the children were sleeping, we went for prayers. We prayed for peace, for the safety of our children and to be able to return home.

The Trùng Khánh Buddhist Temple was situated at the base of a mountain and surrounded by hundreds of acres of rice fields. Originally built in 1924, it had been reconstructed in 1964, when my wife's uncle had discovered a natural cave inside the mountain, behind the temple. He had built a secret passage connecting his praying quarters to this cave and told us that, if the war reached the boundary of the temple, this would be the safest place for my family to hide.

We stayed in the temple for about a month. The children, ranging in age from nineteen to three, were well fed and ran freely in the rice fields, often returning to show me the tiny fish they had caught in the creek. I reminded them that the temple forbade killing even a tiny animal. They quickly forgot the war, but I often ventured into Phan Rang to keep up with events, reassuring Diệu Phương, always the most anxious, that I was only going to buy her favourite baguette.

I always made sure to buy the baguette before I went to the port. Phan Rang was close to Cam Ranh, the main port for the United States Navy so people gathered every day, waiting for a ship to come to transport them to Saigon or even to Guam, the closest American territory.

I often wondered if I should put my entire family on that American ship, if there ever was one. It was impossible to know how much of the news I heard at the port was true, and I hesitated to abandon everything I had achieved in order to take such a risky trip. Besides, each time I returned, the children would greet me cheerfully, exclaiming happily over the baguette. At least for now, they were safe and happy.

My suspicion was confirmed when, after a long day of helping the monks fix the temple storage space and stack more bags of rice in it, my wife told me what she had heard.

"Do you remember the family with six children who arrived at the temple a few days after we settled in?"

I recalled there had been a family with six children who walked several days to get to the temple. "Yes, are they all right? How are the children?"

"They left the temple and went to the port. They heard there was a ship transporting people to the port in Cam Ranh, to get on an American ship. But there was no ship. They waited there for days, until two of their girls got very sick. The family are back and their children are exhausted."

"Are the children okay now? Do they need help?"

"Yes, I looked after their fever."

I stopped venturing to the port, more confident that the decision to keep my family in hiding at the temple was the correct one.

The war slowly revealed itself at the temple gate. More people came to find refuge, but the chief monk only accepted a few. One day a large, pointed rock spontaneously split into two equal pieces with a loud bang, an event many saw as an omen foreshadowing the fall of the South Vietnamese government. A few days later, helicopters were hovering above the temple and gunfights erupted in the rice fields. My wife and I took our children and hid in the secret cave as bullets flew over our heads. We cuddled each other in the cave until nightfall, hearing the bullets shatter the stones on top of the cave. My six younger children were crying, but the three older ones were calm, no doubt remembering all the times we had hidden in the family's cave in Quảng Đức.

People broke down the temple gate to find refuge; dead bodies were found in the rice fields. Finally, North Vietnamese soldiers came to the temple demanding to talk to the chief monk. They asked that the temple provide them with cooked rice and salt.

The children helped the monks cook many oversized rice pots and place them on the steps of the main hall where soldiers arrived each morning and afternoon to politely eat their portion. The children hid behind the statues of Buddha, curious to observe the North Vietnamese soldiers, until they were caught by the monks and asked to leave. Some soldiers reached into their pockets and pulled out a small package that contained some sort of white powder, perhaps monosodium glutamate, that they sprinkled on top, to add more flavour to the plain rice. The children asked me why the soldiers only ate rice with salt and I made up an answer, telling them the North Vietnamese soldiers were vegans.

The soldiers said nothing but acted politely to everyone despite the grenades hanging on their chests and the guns across their shoulders. After each group of soldiers finished their meals, they left and were replaced by others throughout the day. The monks continued with their daily rituals, the rustle of the palm trees mixing with the melancholy sound of the Buddhist mantra.

People started to leave the temple, and the dead bodies were cleared from the rice fields. The North Vietnamese soldiers stopped coming to eat rice. Then, on April 30, 1975, the news was broadcast by radio that the communist soldiers had completely taken over South Vietnam. I kept adjusting the radio antenna, trying to catch the right frequency so that we could piece together broken sentences and understand the distorted voice of the reporter. We learned that the last Americans had left, and the war was officially over.

CHAPTER 6

THE LAND OF MIMOSAS

The flight from Saigon to Đà Lạt only took an hour. My children giggled, playing their trivia game and asking me every few seconds if we were at Đà Lạt yet. They were excited to visit the place that nurtured me from childhood to adolescence, the place where their mother, aunts and uncles once lived happily together, sheltered from a brutal war by their grandparents, only to have all their lives torn apart when it ended. My eyes suddenly filled with bitter tears; I turned toward the window to hide my emotion.

The plane landed safely at Liên Khương airport and I breathed the air of Đà Lạt deep into my lungs. I felt a familiar sense of home and was momentarily confused. My children brought me back to the present.

"Mommy, the weather is cool. The breeze feels the same as Canada," my youngest daughter, Như Thương, said with excitement. At six years of age, she had suffered from heat rash in the hot and humid climate of Saigon and welcomed a move to "the city of fog."

"Mommy, I saw grass, green grass. And there is the mountain shaped like an elephant," said my second daughter, Hoàng Thương. She was only two years older than her sister but loved to read. She had taken her research seriously and learned about Elephant Mountain, *Núi Voi*, visible from the foot of the plateau, and its association with a story of forbidden love. The shape of the elephant, its front feet forever kneeling, mourns the tragic deaths of two lovers.

43

"Mom, did we get all the luggage? Mom, I saw the hotel driver. He's holding up a sign with your last name," my oldest daughter, Diệu Thương, reminded me. At seventeen, she felt a deep sense of responsibility for her two younger sisters. I often wondered if she had inherited my worried nature and carried part of my sorrow. I had given her my middle name without thinking too much about the Buddhist theology behind it.

We headed toward the hotel driver, who held a sign reading "Hoàng." I looked at the sign and was overcome with a flood of mixed emotion. Twenty-five years ago, I left this place in secret, to flee my country, avoiding most people, afraid they would guess our escape plan. Now, everyone around me was happily greeting their relatives, and a stranger was holding a sign with my last name. I stopped moving, lost in an old reality.

Father meticulously arranged trips for all of us to leave Đà Lạt in small groups, weeks apart, to avoid suspicion. My older siblings went to Saigon with Father first. Then Mother took Lan Phương and my three younger brothers, Phi, Phổ and Phấn, out of school saying Grandmother was ill, which was true, except that they were not going to visit her. Instead, Father returned to accompany them to Saigon. The evening before they left, Father handed me a note saying I also needed to take a few days off to travel to Mũi Né to visit my grandmother.

"Jolie, I will come back to take you to Saigon in ten days." In the meantime, I was to stay with my oldest sister, Mỹ Phương. She had been married for six years and now had three young children ranging from four years to one month old. Her family had decided to remain in Vietnam.

Father gently reminded me, "Hold on to this note. Only hand it to your homeroom teacher the day before you leave Đà Lạt."

I had started to lose interest in school a few years ago, when Phú had left Đà Lạt to help Father with the escape plan. My remaining days at school now seemed completely pointless. I was tired of starting each day by reading aloud political slogans that praised the heroes from the North. I had had enough of learning how the communist soldiers of North Vietnam had liberated us, ending years of war and destruction at the hands of the American invaders. I didn't say anything to anyone, but I suspected my classmates would guess my secret the day I stopped showing up for class.

After school each day, I prepared to leave. I played my guitar and sang myself a song about Đà Lạt, a secret goodbye to the city of my childhood. I rode my bicycle on various roads and hills, thinking it would be the last time. I visited the library and stopped by the church with the rooster on top. I rode to my old French private school, Hùng Vương. The red, European-style building had been converted to a teacher training college where Phiên had been studying. I let my bicycle roll freely down the slope of a street where mimosas bloomed on both sides. I nodded a silent farewell to the bright yellow flowers that represented secret love and were also an emblem of femininity and freedom. I was struck by the contrast between this symbol of freedom and the reality of our daily life. As I pedalled along, the gentle breeze carried with it the scents of pine and sweet acacia. I grieved my impending loss of my home even as I found myself desperately wanting to leave Đà Lạt, to be free from uncertainty and a life weighted with secrecy. The early morning fog and the afternoon rain became increasingly oppressive as the days passed.

The ten long days of waiting were finally over. Father returned and bought me a small blue Puma bag, telling me to pack only essential personal belongings. He told me the weather would be hot so I would not need to pack any sweaters, the one that I would wear to leave Đà Lạt would be enough. We left quietly without waking the others and walked to the bus station in thick fog that concealed our departure. It was too early for any of the usual morning activities, so the street was quiet, and we walked fast, in silence.

As we approached the bus station, the hectic morning activity began, slowly dissipated the fog. A soft breeze blew the tiny droplets of a rare morning drizzle against our faces, cooling the air around us and leaving a thin layer of moisture on Father's sunglasses. We stopped at a street stall and Father bought me *xôi vò,* sticky rice with mung bean wrapped in fresh banana leaves. Then he bought a mango from an older lady walking around the bus station, her baskets supported by a bamboo rod hung across her shoulders. He peeled off the skin and handed it to me gently.

The sun was on the horizon as the bus pulled away from the station, slowly turning into a narrow road crowded with street stalls and filled with people riding their bicycles and pedestrians in a hurry. I told myself not to turn my head, to never look back, to leave all the images, all the memories of Đà Lạt behind me.

"Mommy, hurry, why are you stopping? Did you forget something?" My children turned around, grasped my hands and pulled me toward the driver holding the sign.

I wanted to tell them that I needed to forget, right at this moment, the fear, the feeling of loss I had felt when I tried to escape this place, not knowing whether death or freedom lay ahead. But the moment passed and I moved toward our driver with determination.

As we approached the city of Đà Lạt, the road turned up a steep hill, climbing to the plateau. My children pulled out their cameras and started taking pictures of the green mountain, its top obscured by clouds.

"Mommy, are we going to go into those clouds?" Như Thương asked.

"Yes, we can see them from here, but when we are in them, we won't be able to."

"Why not, Mommy?"

I recalled asking my father the same question as he drove my siblings and me up these steep, swirling hills in his green Jeep Cherokee. How did he answer that question? I tried to remember, but my mind was blank.

We checked into the Du Parc Hotel, located near Xuân Hương Lake, at nightfall. My daughters fell asleep immediately, tired from the excitement and the time difference, but I remained half-awake, half-asleep. Hovering on the edge of consciousness, I held onto the hope that I would see my father in my dream again, that his warm smile would soothe my heart. But no dream came, despite my longing.

CHAPTER 7

PEACE AND FIRE

Now that the fighting had stopped, we left the temple and drove home to find our house untouched. The children returned to school and we re-opened the pharmacy. But nothing would be the same.

South Vietnamese officials and those who worked for the Americans were sent to prisons for "political reformation." Children brought forms home from school and were required to list their family background. Families with relatives who had worked for the previous government, landowners and wealthy merchants were labelled "bad elements." Many were forced out of their homes and into "new economic zones." Their homes and property were confiscated and given to communist officials.

The new government introduced a currency exchange. All citizens had to turn in their old bills in return for a set amount of North Vietnamese money, regardless of how much they turned in. My wife sat on the bed, staring at the piles of South Vietnamese currency, most of them royal blue and bearing the image of Royal Prince Trần Hưng Đạo, a brilliant military strategist who had twice repulsed Mongolian invaders. The bills bearing his image were the highest denomination available, now suddenly worthless. I prepared a fire at the back of the house and burned it all, keeping only enough to meet the required amount of exchange. Any excess would add to our risk of being labelled a bad element. We watched the flames in silence, periodically stirring the ashes with iron pokers, ensuring no trace of royal blue remained.

A year later, the pharmacy and the green Jeep Cherokee were confiscated. Then communist policemen came to my home trying to find my gold. Grenades no longer decorated their green shirts, but they wore pistols at their waist. The children were all home, terrified and huddled together on one bed. My wife didn't say a word and I tried to remain calm, but my blood was boiling on the inside. I resolved that, as soon as they demanded to search my children, I would grab their guns and fight back, no matter what. However, they were not violent and I baited them with obvious things that they busily took away. They were reasonably satisfied with the telephone, the typewriter, the fridge and the television. While the soldiers picked and chose what they wanted, our pet dog, Milou, barked aggressively, its tongue sticking out, dripping with saliva, exposing its sharp teeth. The neighbour's dog joined in and together they expressed what their owners could not. It was legalized theft in broad daylight.

The next day, I was summoned to the central police station, and told they wanted my family dog. My next-door neighbour was also summoned and told to turn in his dog, even though his home had not been searched and none of his assets were confiscated.

I came home not knowing what to tell my children. Strangely, they reported that both dogs had kept to themselves in the corners of their houses all day, making sad sounds and refusing to play. I wondered how they knew. The policemen arrived before I could prepare my children and, in front all of them, tied the dogs, one by one, on a leash. The children cried. The dogs wailed. Tears were running from the children's eyes, from the dogs' and from mine as well. The policemen decided to muzzle the animals. The dogs knew the end of their lives had arrived and refused to leave, spreading their legs in resistance. Their paws made shrieking sounds and left long scratches on the cement as they were dragged away. I told all the children to go inside the house, but they went running after the animals, screaming.

They had lost their television and their fridge and had not shed a tear, but my children cried for their pet dog for months, as did the neighbour's children. I tried to comfort them by reminding them that, according to Buddhist belief, when animals die, they are re-incarnated as humans, but this did not relieve their pain.

Next, the local communist officials decided that books published and sheet music for songs composed under the South Vietnamese government had to be burned or destroyed. Each household had to bring their books to an assigned location in the city. My wife helped the children sort the books we had collected over the years and together they burned the political and history books at the back of the house. Once again, they tended the fire, making sure every single page turned entirely to ashes. But there were too many books to burn and it seemed unlikely that we would be searched again. My wife decided that we would hide the rest. Later, when paper became a rare commodity, we tore pages from those books for our daily needs.

But, for all we lost, the authorities never found my gold. My wife sewed ingots into the lining of our clothes, and the children wore them without knowing. We gathered rare medicines and hid them throughout the house, between the ceiling and the roof, under the mattress where my youngest daughter slept and in a particular corner of the kitchen. That hidden gold and those rare medicines helped my family survive for years.

CHAPTER 8

THE ROOSTER

The Du Parc hotel is located next to Đà Lạt Cathedral, a Catholic church that is a remnant of the French occupation. We could see it from the window of our hotel and my daughters pointed out the carved rooster on the top of the church tower. "Why is the rooster there, Mommy?"

I remembered asking the same question when I was about six.

The answer my father had given me was the one I chose to give to my children. "It has to be a rooster. If it were a chicken, then it would lay eggs that might land on someone's head." My daughters laughed and I laughed with them, momentarily rooted in childhood memories. Mother had wanted him to explain that churches displayed the rooster on their steeples as a reminder that Simon Peter, one of the twelve apostles, had disowned Jesus Christ three times before the rooster crowed, something Jesus has predicted and Peter bitterly repented. The rooster crowing at dawn signified the triumph of light over darkness, resurrection over death. My father knew all this but didn't share it until years later, preferring to amuse his children and tease his wife.

At the end of each day, my children were exhausted from so much sightseeing, especially from walking up and down the steep hills. But I was energized by all the streets we explored, each of which bore the imprint of my childhood. On the streets of this charming city, breathing its mountainous air, even meeting many strangers, I still felt entirely at home. Walking back to the hotel one evening, Diệu Thương took some pictures of the church, whose beautiful setting made it a popular subject for many photographers. Hoàng Thương and Như Thương happily jumped up and down the front steps, their laughter echoing against the church walls, while I enjoyed the pleasant evening breeze and remembered a photograph of Father sitting on the bench in front of this church. For over thirty years, through days of war and peace, this church had stood tall, its rooster still on its roof, connecting three generations.

Nearby, members of the congregation were raising funds by selling beautiful hand-knitted sweaters, each delicately crafted with elegant patterns using the soft colours of the flowers of Đà Lạt. I bought a few for the girls but searched in vain for a lavender one for me.

Mother was a career-oriented woman and devoted mother. I was four when we moved to Đà Lạt and she began her career at the pharmacy. At first, two cousins, Chị Khuê and Chị Huyên, came from Huế to help take care of us while Father and Mother worked. And each morning, before she left for work, Mother assigned specific tasks to all of us, making it clear that we were not to rely on them entirely. When the sisters returned to their hometown to get married, the older siblings took turns taking care of the younger ones the way I would one day look after Lan Phương.

It was the delicate thread of yarn that knotted us together. In keeping with long-standing tradition, my mother was taught to knit by her mother, and it was a skill she continued to develop throughout her life. She was blessed with a modern father who allowed her to pursue higher education and my mother found knitting helped relieve stress. During the three years of nursing school, she joined a knitting group, making socks, hats and baby sweaters for the infant ward during her night shifts.

Mother continued to knit during whatever free time her busy life allowed; we often helped by rolling the yarns and blending the colours according to our own tastes. She taught her daughters to knit, and our cousins Chị Khuê and Chị Huyên also learned from Mother. They used to knit sweaters for themselves whenever they had free time, but I never saw them finish any. Once Mother began operating the pharmacy at Trại Mát, a basket of yarn and partially finished sweaters was always behind the counter in case she had any spare time.

When I turned eight, Mother knitted me a special sweater in a pattern she designed herself, a complex cable one shaped like the pine trees of Đà Lạt. She knew that, of all her children, I would most appreciate the delicacy and symbolism, so she drew a chart to calculate the required number of stitches. She also knew that my favourite colour was purple, but Grandmother had told her that purple symbolized the tragedy and misery of a woman betrayed by her true love, so she chose lavender instead.

"Jolie, I know you like purple, but lavender goes better with your skin tone." It would be years before she told me the real reason.

She was worried I would be disappointed, but I was so happy I wore that sweater almost every day. I loved the soft stitches and the criss-crossed pattern. When I grew out of it, I reused the yarn to make a sweater for Lan Phương.

Mother made sweaters for all my siblings. She knew all our favourite colours and made us each something unique and special, a wordless demonstration of her love.

CHAPTER 9

THE OIL LAMP

Darkness descended. The busy roads were quieter with no street-lights; the sound of a barking dog resonated in the cold air. Another night without power in this part of the city—the communist government had divided Đà Lạt into several districts, each of which had no electricity for two consecutive days each week. People withdrew inside their homes, behind their steel front doors.

Phiên slid our front door shut, shaking the lock to make sure it was secure. The sound of clanking metal broke the unnerving silence. Three oil lamps in the kitchen gave just enough light to cook our meal. I had also placed an oil lamp in each room so the children would not have to carry lamps with them. I worried they could drop them and cause a fire. The last lamp was for the dinner table.

"Jolie, why don't you clean the glass chimney?" This was a chore she took pride in doing well.

"Yes, Father!"

She carefully cleaned the inside of the chimney with a cloth tied around an old chopstick until it was spotless while Phú helped me pour more oil into the font. I dipped the wick into the oil and pulled it through the burner socket. I made sure they were both paying attention. "Look at this wick. It needs to be pulled through the socket, but only enough to burn without smoking."

I touched my cigarette lighter to the wick and watched the fire follow the oil around the circular wick to form a perfect circumference. Jolie attached the now spotless glass chimney and adjusted the knob.

Mouth-watering scents of garlic, onion and oil filled the room as Hằng Phương announced that dinner was ready. She had helped her mother prepare our three main dishes: squash soup, stir-fried vegetables and stewed fish. As she arranged the dishes on the table, I asked Phú to place the oil lamp near me so that I could pick all the bones out of the fish. "I think on the days without electricity, we should not buy fish. They have so many tiny bones."

"This kind of fish is the only kind that is available lately," my wife replied, "and pork is so difficult to find these days."

The children began to eat. My wife and I ate sparingly, thinking of the next meal. We lived day to day, with enough food on the table, but not knowing what the communist government would do to our family. I had bribed the officials to keep our home and my family in Đà Lạt and had been successful so far, but that could change at any moment.

Privately, I complained to my wife that the policies of the new government were as changeable as the weather. "This morning it was sunny. Then in the afternoon, the sky suddenly poured rain. It is like this government. Today, we are allowed to have some peace and normalcy. But tomorrow, the communist officials could suddenly storm into our home, charge us with the crime of bribery and force us to leave. It has happened to other families."

She was also worried. "I hear the new economic zones are full of infested forests and contaminated water. Some families have decided to return, preferring to be homeless. I have seen children with swollen bellies; their parents ask me to treat their diseases. But swollen bellies do not result from illness. They come from malnutrition."

We often talked long into the night, trying to figure out what to do for the future of our ten children. But during the evening, we did our best to maintain a normal and happy family life. After dinner, once homework and chores had been completed, I would gather the whole family on our bed and ask each of the children about their studies and compliment them on their achievements. My wife and I were amazed with their creativity and talents in music as well as in literature and science.

Once our meeting concluded, I often agreed to play the tiger game. The children divided themselves into two groups, each hiding under a blanket. My role was to be a tiger in search of food. I crawled around, making fierce tiger sounds and using my "paws" to try to get under the blankets. When I was successful, I tickled my prey.

After the children were in bed, I watched the light burning inside the shining oil lamp and wondered if our current life could be compared to this flame. A flame that burned with only enough fuel to give light, not warmth, and one that could be extinguished at any time.

CHAPTER 10

THE RICE CHEST

I took my daughters to visit my old home, now occupied by a woman I did not know who operated a small boutique specializing in men's shirts out of the living room. I trembled as I stood in front of the house, seeing the younger me and my siblings playing with the next-door neighbour's children as my parents came home wearing coats soaked from the usual afternoon rain. The two houses were still there, standing on the same spot, sharing a common wall and a long stretch of aluminum roof. But where were the people? The next-door neighbour's children had grown and moved away; their home also belonged to someone else.

"Mommy, is this your old house?" asked Như Thương.

"Most of the houses here have no front lawn. Is this where you played with our uncles and aunts?" asked Hoàng Thương.

"Mom, can we go inside? Maybe we can buy something here," Diệu Thương suggested.

My daughters pulled me inside the house and started inspecting the merchandise, which seemed invisible to me. I was looking at the spot where my small desk used to be, near the altar of family ancestors, my favourite place to complete my homework, the air often redolent with incense. There used to be a guitar hanging on the wall nearby in the rare moments one of us was not playing it. My heart sank, remembering Lan Phương singing while I played the chords.

"May I help you?" I heard the voice of the owner, louder than usual.

"Mom, the lady has already asked you the same thing three times," Diệu Thương reminded me.

"I am sorry. I was lost for a second. To be honest, I used to live in this house," I explained in Vietnamese. She did not reply.

"Can we see more of the house, Mommy?" asked Như Thương in English.

"Can we see your bedroom, Mom?" asked Hoàng Thương, also in English.

Their language puzzled the lady of the house.

I turned back to the lady. "I am sorry for intruding. I used to live in this house. My daughters ask if they can see the rest."

The lady was not happy. "Why do people keep asking to see this house? For the past few years, there is someone almost every year."

I realized why she frowned. "I have eight siblings who have come back to visit Vietnam before me. Perhaps they asked for the same thing I just did."

She reluctantly agreed that we could walk through the house as long as we did it quickly and left right after.

Everything was different. I could only point to where the beds had been, two for all my brothers and another for me and my sisters. What had been our living room had been turned into space for selling the merchandise. The bathroom and the kitchen maintained their original layouts, but there was no longer a back door that led to the small, open area with the ladder we used to climb up onto the aluminum roof. The ceiling had been repaired, covering the corner where my parents hid their medicines and their gold. I wondered if the current owner knew about that spot. Strangest of all, the rice chest was gone. I wondered how they had managed to move it.

Father bought the chest in 1972, soon after we moved to Đà Lạt. He brought the pieces home in his green Jeep Cherokee and we were all excited to help him carry them into the kitchen. Then we sat beside him for hours, watching him assemble it. It was made with sliding covers and divided into three compartments, each of which was large enough to fit three of us.

"Father, what are we going to put inside this big chest?" We were all so curious.

"I plan to put plenty of rice in at least two compartments."

"Can we call it the rice chest?"

"Of course, call it the rice chest. But in the other compartment, we will store fish sauce, dried produce and dried fish." Father showed us how to slide the tops closed without getting our fingers caught. The rice chest would also serve as a bench for my three younger brothers at the dining table.

Father planned to keep the chest full of rice to keep us from hunger in case of hard times. In the other compartment, he kept provisions brought by Grandmother or Uncle Phát whenever they visited us from Mũi Né, a town famous for its seafood and delicate fish sauce. After 1975, the rice compartments were never filled to the top. There was, eventually, only enough to fill one quarter of one compartment. Most of the time we could not reach the rice; one of us had to climb in. The preserved fish sauce, dried squid and dried fish were also soon depleted.

We got rice using the food stamps each family received from the government. On a specific day of each week, we lined up, presented our food stamps and receive our portion. The rice evolved from white to yellow, then became diluted with economical kinds of wheat. Portions kept getting smaller until we only received enough rice to cook a few pots. Other elements of the food chain slowly vanished until what we once took for granted was remembered as a luxury of the past.

When the rice chest was empty, it served as a hiding place for our games of hide and seek, except it was such an obvious place to hide. So, on the nights we had no electricity, we invented a new game with the rice chest, a modified version of hide and seek. My brothers would hide inside; I would use my hands to identify them by feeling their heads. I cheated once, tickling their necks so that they laughed and gave themselves away. Each time we played, Lan Phương and I could not stop laughing.

Time passed. We got older and could no longer fit three inside one compartment. After Phán left for Saigon and Phú went to help Father with his boat business, there were no more games of modified hide and seek. Now the rice chest was only used to hide forbidden books: the biography of Chopin, the fairy tales of Hans Christian Andersen and others I secretly exchanged with some of my close friends at school, hiding them under my oversize raincoat, running home and reading them while the doors remained locked.

The rice chest had triggered a feeling of hollowness each time I looked at it, missing the laughter of my brothers. It was so substantial but so awfully bare, lacking the rich mixed smell of rice, fish sauce, dried squids and fried codfish.

I bought two men's shirts to express my thanks to the new owner. Looking at the displays, neatly folded or hanging to attract customers, I remembered the closet in which my father kept all the shirts I carefully ironed for him, gently steaming out all the wrinkles.

CHAPTER 11

A Postcard from Germany

As our daily life became more difficult, I spent more and more time secretly listening to the news on my small radio, switching between the distorted voices of the reporters from the British Broadcasting Corporation and Voice of America. The communist government had banned all channels broadcasting news from outside Vietnam, especially those sharing stories of people escaping the country and being rescued by huge foreign vessels in international waters.

The first emigrants had been wealthy citizens, and the new communist government wanted access to the substantial riches they had stashed away. They left Vietnam in an orderly fashion in well-built boats, having purchased exit visas with their hidden diamonds or gold bars. Others, many from the new economic zone who couldn't afford the exit permits, followed, escaping illegally. Those who were captured were thrown into prison, their assets confiscated. When they were released, they became criminals and were often banished to the new economic zones. No one mentioned the escapees who were never heard from again.

A new phrase, "*vượt biên*," was invented: *vượt* meant escaping or passing across, and *biên* meant border. *Vượt biên*—illegally leaving Vietnam—was added to the criminal code. People only whispered these words; no one dared utter them out loud. If they were overheard, they could be charged with high treason. Ironically, for many citizens, *vượt biên* also signified hope when their lives in their home-land became unbearable.

One day, Phán showed me a postcard he had received from a friend, a postcard from Germany. When this friend had suddenly stopped coming to school, no one asked about him, no one alerted the school officials, nothing had been said. Now we knew their escape had been successful.

I borrowed the postcard from Phán and stayed up the entire night looking at it, overwhelmed by the freedom, the opportunities now available to the young man who had sent it. It could happen for my children too. I decided to make it happen. The postcard was the catalyst that began a new and even more dangerous phase of our family life.

The government controlled most commodities, and necessary daily supplies, including medicine, were increasingly hard to find. Both over-the-counter and prescription drugs were secretly traded out of people's homes, including ours. I travelled frequently, some-times for months, to buy rare medicines on the black market in Saigon, concealing my purchases in the lining of my coat or inside a secret compartment in my small travel bag. My trips also included searching for contacts who could arrange for our escape.

My wife sometimes accompanied me. Eventually, we went to Cần Thơ, the largest city on the Mekong Delta, to meet a reliable source who connected people with those who arranged the escapes. We attended a secret meeting where we heard thorough details of the plan, then we visited the vessel that would be used. We became convinced, placed our trust in their plan and used a significant por-tion of our gold to buy seats for Phiên, Phán and Phú.

When we returned, I had a private conversation with all three boys. Phiên reacted cautiously, while Phán was enthusiastic. Phú was calm and paid careful attention as I explained the details.

Overwhelmed by the enormity of what we were proposing, my wife retired to our bedroom while I gathered the rest of the family together. "For the next little while, Phiên, Phán and Phú will be away from home. Whenever anyone asks about their absence, just say that they are at Mũi Né visiting your grandmother."

I made my voice as serious as I could, trying to impress on all the children, even the youngest, how important this was. "If people start to interrogate you or try to intimidate you with the words *vượt biên*, then stay calm. Just tell them that you don't know what they are talking about. The best thing to do is to ignore them and walk away. Make sure you tell me right after, about what has happened, with whom and when." The atmosphere was tense, heavy with unasked questions. They understood the situation and remained silent.

We secretly left in the middle of the night a few days later, avoiding goodbyes. I waited in Saigon as my sons travelled on to Cần Thơ. They were secretly brought to a spot near a fishing port where they gathered with some other escapees. Just as they were to go to where they could board the boat, they heard a scream that seemed to come from nowhere, "Police! Police! Run! Run for your life! Or you will be captured and put in prison!"

They ran as fast as they could and hid in a nearby supermarket until dark, then found their way back to Saigon by bus the next day. They stayed with me at a hotel in Saigon for two more days before I sent them home. I stayed behind to try to find out what was going on.

The whole thing had been a setup. There had been no boat to escape in, and no policemen waiting to catch the escapees. It was a wicked scam, taking advantage of the desperate. I went to Cần Thơ to try to retrieve my lost gold but the organizers had disappeared, taking my ingots with them. I felt outraged and anguished but I couldn't tell anyone. If I exposed the scheme, I could be arrested too. After I returned to Đà Lạt, the disaster led to a rare argument with my wife, who withdrew to her room and stayed in bed for days, whimpering softly.

Slowly, I got over my disappointment. At least my sons had come back alive. The scammers could have arranged for a non-functional boat and taken the escapees a short distance into the rough sea. Their lives could have been lost before they were ever caught and imprisoned.

CHAPTER 12

FEAST FOR THE DEAD

The day we visited my old home, I noticed that the shortcut to the temple was still intact. It had even been enhanced with a beautiful mixture of red and purple bougainvillea glabra planted on both sides. We stopped to admire and take pictures of the flowers in full bloom. Then I led my children along the path to the temple, where we lit incense and prayed in the main hall. I showed them the spot near the bell tower, where Lan Phương and I used to sit, pray and act out our plays. I remembered the tortoises.

"Back then, when I was little, there were many tortoises who lived around a man-made lotus pond at this temple. After prayers, Father would take me and my siblings to the back of the main hall to see them. But after 1975, all the turtles were gone. Let's see if the lotus pond is still there."

We walked to the back of the main hall and stepped through a door that used to lead to the lotus pond, but it was no longer there. Instead, we found a well-cultivated garden filled with many types of vegetables.

"Were they big? Were there lots of them, Mommy?" asked Như Thương. From a a very young age, she'd shown a distinct fondness for animals.

"Yes, they were huge, Asian Giant Tortoises with Buddhist characters or Buddhist symbols on their shells. I saw quite a few of them. The monks said the big ones were at least thirty years old."

"Why did the monks engrave Buddhist symbols on their shells, Mommy?" asked Hoàng Thương, as questioning and precise as ever.

"I think they did that to let people know that the tortoises belonged to the temple. We all called them the temple turtles: *Rùa đi tu.*"

"Would it hurt when the monk engraved the Buddhist symbols on them?" asked Như Thương, sounding worried.

I recalled asking my father the same question. I repeated the answer he gave to us. "No, absolutely not. The etching was a few millimetres deep and barely marked the shell. It certainly didn't touch the sensitive bone beneath."

"Is it the same concept as the monks shaving their heads?" asked Hoàng Thương, her logical mind wanting to learn more about the Buddhist theology. Both Như Thương and Diệu Thương giggled.

"Yes. I think so." I answered her, trying to hide my own laugh.

"Why tortoises, Mom? Can other animals live at the temple too? Maybe a cat?" asked Diệu Thương. She loved cats.

"Yes, I think so. But there is more to it. The tortoise carries a heavy shell and is also a peaceful animal. Their stamina reflects the acceptance of fate, peacefulness and forgiveness. It carries in itself a Buddhism spirit. They're my favourite animal."

"What happened to them, Mommy?" asked Như Thương.

I hesitated. Diệu Thương watched me, knowing I was trying to find the right answer.

"You said they were gone after 1975. Why, Mommy?" asked Hoàng Thương.

"I really don't know. I wanted to know what happened too. I asked your grandfather the same question but he did not know the answer either."

I decided to change the topic. "There used to be a vast tea field here too. I often wandered past it after school. Many times, I plucked the tea leaves and the flower sprouts and ate them." Now the land was filled with houses, many of them with shared walls.

"Did they taste bitter, Mommy?" asked Như Thương.

"At the time I thought they tasted quite sweet." I recalled the taste clearly, even after more than thirty years.

"Weren't you afraid of getting caught? Did the monks catch you?" asked Hoàng Thương, intrigued by the idea of her mother doing something secret.

"No, I never got caught."

"Now we know why you are addicted to tea!" Diệu Thương said.

All three of my daughters laughed, and so did I. But my laughter was mixed with bitter tears as I heard the echo of Lan Phương's giggles.

We walked back into the main hall, breathing cool air blended with the pleasant smell of incense. Then we stopped in front of giant brass incense burner that still stood in front of the main temple hall—a reminder of a particularly dark time.

I woke up one morning to find that Father and my three older brothers had left in the middle of the night. There were no words of goodbye since we had to keep the plan a complete secret. We all felt uneasy and extremely sad, but Mother reminded us to act normal—it was a matter of life and death.

"Chị Jolie, where is Anh Phú?" asked Lan Phương.

I tried to ignore her but she kept asking. She was used to him helping me take care of her. The third time she asked, her voice rising, I told her what Father had instructed. "Anh Phú has gone to Mũi Né to visit Grandmother."

"Why didn't he say anything?" asked Lan Phương in a doubtful tone. She was brilliant and also quite sensitive, qualities that often come in pairs.

I gently covered her mouth. "Father wanted us to keep this quiet for a while." I knew that as soon as I mentioned Father's instructions, she would understand.

I went to school that day and sat in class, but every word the teacher said bounced off my head. I tried to keep my eyes trained on the blackboard but retained nothing from the lessons. Another tense day passed, then a third, even more stressful day. I started to feel that I would need to adapt to this new type of anxiety, on top of all the existing ones.

"Chị Jolie!" Lan Phương greeted me eagerly as I arrived home. "Anh Phiên, Anh Phán and Anh Phú came home this afternoon. Anh Phú said Father will be home in a few days. Anh Phán said he did not have time to walk to the beach to find us any seashells." Her innocence lightened the mixture of disappointment and relief the rest of us were feeling. "Maybe Father will bring us some."

Whenever Father came home from a long trip, he brought us little gifts. One time, the gifts were seashells. Mine was a huge triton shell. Father told me to hold it to my ear so I could hear the sound of the ocean, explaining that when the creature left its shell, it left its spirit behind to mourn its passing, its cry like the sound of the ocean. He told me every creature has a spirit and the fact that animals can't talk doesn't mean that they cannot feel pain. As human beings, together, we need to respect nature and should not take it for granted.

My brothers resumed their usual daily routine, saying nothing about what had happened. Our simple meals became silent and the food seemed tasteless as we waited for Father to come home. We were so happy when he appeared at the end of a long week. But the warmth was gone from his smile. There was no seashell or other present for Lan Phương, only an air of despondency that lasted for days. He didn't initiate playful family gatherings as he used to; he just reminded us to concentrate on our homework. Father became less present—he began to take longer, more frequent trips and seemed tense whenever he was home, listening to the radio in his room. One night, Mother pulled out her tin sewing box and altered the lining of Father's coat. The next day, we came home from school on a rainy afternoon to find that he had left without a word. Mother said that he had to travel far, to a town near the Mekong river, to find a way to change our future.

Mother and Hằng Phương cooked fewer dishes. Produce was harder to buy and the huge dining table looked empty. There were even more days with no electricity. Once taken for granted as a necessity of daily life, it had become a rare privilege, even a luxury. Phú and I prepared the oil lamps alone, missing Father's gentle voice explaining the science.

We all missed Father and tried to concentrate on our school tasks. On a particularly rainy afternoon, we shut the steel front door and sat at our desks. Lan Phương was sitting beside me, practising her hand-writing, when we heard a loud knock. Over the sound of the rain, a familiar voice said, "Children! Open the door for me. I'm home!"

We all dropped everything and saw our father in a huge raincoat. He was in his middle fifties but had few white hairs, and the sun-glasses he habitually wore made him look younger and handsomely cool. He was wet and cold, and his face looked skinnier, but his smile held the old warmth. That night we lingered at dinner, surrounded by laughter, my brothers sitting on the empty rice chest.

I wished Father would stay home forever, but he left again soon after. The day before, we were told that a guest from out of town would be joining us. Father never told us who he was, perhaps to keep his identity safe. Mother prepared a special supper and we set an extra dinner plate. The guest arrived, soaked from the heavy rain, and removed a large amount of currency from his pocket. He placed the wet bills on the counter and on the lid of the rice pot to dry while we ate dinner. Afterward, Father made sure the steel door was tightly shut and that all the holes in the wall we shared with our next-door neighbour were completely covered. Father and the man conversed in whispers until past midnight. The next morning, the mysterious guest left with Father and Mother, without any explanation for us.

Grandmother came to Đà Lạt to take care of us and insisted we make a special feast for the dead. Traditionally, on the fifteenth of July according to the lunar calendar, every household paid respect to the dead who did not have a proper burial and had no relative to remember or light incense for them. Grandmother said these spirits roamed the earth, crying their hearts out, but no human could hear them.

Before 1975, Father and Mother conscientiously performed this ritual on the traditional day in July, first at their pharmacy in Trại Mát around noon and then in the evening at our home in Đà Lạt. But the declaration of peace in Vietnam had largely ended the feast for the dead; communist officials monitored temples, and people who attended services were "red flagged," marked as potential threats to government policy. It was a tactic intended to silence alternative thinking and beliefs.

I accompanied Grandmother on a visit her distant cousin to order a chicken for the ritual to honour the dead. He later arrived at our front door with a squawking chicken he said was old and could no longer lay eggs. The chicken was trapped inside a bamboo basket secured with a lid, but still flapped its wings vigorously, trying to free itself, shredding a lot of its feathers in the process. I thought of Father and Mother, off on their mysterious journey. Seeking freedom is natural for any living creature.

We kept the chicken alive for more than a week, feeding it with some rice at every meal; we even gave it a name. When the time came to kill Ngố, none of us wanted to help Grandmother. Killing and preparing a chicken is not easy, and we gave her all kinds of excuses. She was surprised by our behaviour and frustrated by our stubbornness. In the end, she had to ask our father's nephew-in-law, Thiện, to help.

The featherless chicken was boiled with its head still attached and its eyes open. Then it was placed on a plate and put on a small table in front of the house, with side dishes and a cup of rice to hold the incense upright. The chicken's skin rippled with fat under the shining moonlight, ready to be offered to the roaming ghosts. Grandmother carefully lit the incense and respectfully kowtowed nine times in four directions: north, east, south and west. She placed herself directly in front of the chicken to kowtow again, in the direction of the west, pausing and praying with a burning stick of incense held between the tips of her fingers.

She performed the ritual for two purposes: to pay respect to the dead and to ask for a blessing. She knew about the plan, the plan to escape Vietnam. Would the sacrifice of this chicken be enough to activate the mysterious power of the dead, to bless us with luck to gain our freedom in the land of the west?

The entire neighbourhood was quiet on that night of the full moon. No one offered a feast for the dead except for our family. Phú, Phi, Phổ, Phấn and I took turns guarding the offering table. The night was cold and the wind gently carried the smell of incense, a pleasant scent to invite the ghosts to feast on the chicken. I felt a chill down my spine, imagining all kinds of invisible spirits gathered around the table. It was scary to think that they could see me but I could not see them, and I wanted one of my brothers to stay with me. However, there came a moment when I was guarding the table alone.

Suddenly, a dirty head poked up from behind the table: "Boo…!" I fell off my chair and screamed. Phú, Phi, Phổ and Phấn immediately ran from the back of the house to check on me. I was crying, frightened to my bones, convinced I had just seen a spirit who could talk.

"The chicken is gone!" all my brothers screamed at the same time. Grandmother came running out.

"A thief has stolen the chicken!"

"He cannot have run far. Jolie, did you see what direction he went?" asked Phú.

Still crying, I answered, "I didn't see where he was running. I thought it was a ghost."

Grandmother comforted me. "There, there, Jolie, a ghost would not be able to run away with the chicken. It was a thief who scared you in order to steal it." She shook her head. "It is bad luck! The incense is still burning, not even half burned."

Grandmother turned to Phú. "Do not run after the thief. It is dangerous. He must be far away by now."

Around the dinner table that evening, everyone was quiet, with grumpy faces, thinking about the chicken and its delicious meat, which we could have feasted on after asking for a blessing from the dead. Instead, we only had the soup Grandmother had made from the broth.

For the rest of the evening, Grandmother kept shaking her head, and finally said, "These days, hardly anyone prepares a feast to offer the dead. Such a shame! What has become of this world? People and even kids steal food from the dead."

I thought about losing the chicken for a long time, trying to remember the face that popped up from behind the table. I thought it seemed familiar. Who dared to steal food from the dead? Was he not afraid of the invisible world's power?

When they returned, we told Father and Mother about the chicken thief. Mother looked at Father and said, "Do you think he is from the family your niece was telling us about? She said one body was missing."

Father signalled Mother not to say anything else in front of us. It had to be a horrendous story that he did not want us to hear. But we had already heard most of it from the neighbour's children.

The boy's family had been very wealthy, his parents both land-owners and merchants. His uncles had worked for the previous government and were imprisoned in the re-education camps. These factors put his family at the top of the "bad element" list. Their lands and wealth were seized and the family was shipped to the new economic zone, where they were reduced to eating leaves and bugs. After his mother and his sisters died from eating manioc leaves, the boy and his surviving family had returned to Đà Lạt. His father broke into one of the houses that he used to own, now occupied by a high-ranking communist official who was away on vacation. The father gathered what was left of his family, his sons, and together they committed suicide by drinking weed killer they found in the house. The official returned from his trip to find the dead bodies of the previous owner's family. While tracking the corpses' names through their family dossier, he discovered that the chicken thief was missing. He had escaped the suicide pact and defied the tragedy of his family to survive.

"He went to the same school as our cousins," the neighbour's children had told us. "He hangs out at the market during the day. At night, he sleeps inside the gigantic brass incense burner in the temple."

I looked at my parents, finally sharing my fear. "I heard that anyone who stole food from the dead would be mysteriously punished."

Mother rolled her eyes. "Jolie, who told you that? Take that idea out of your head!"

Father gathered our attention. "Jolie, all of you, listen to me. Losing the chicken is not important. The main point here is the homeless boy is less hungry. I will check with the chief monk of the temple to see if he has seen the boy and given him shelter."

The chief monk told Father he did not know what had happened to the homeless boy who once slept in the incense burner. The child had vanished from the temple grounds and no one knew where he had gone.

The bell at Linh Sơn Temple still rings on the first and the fifteenth of each month according to the lunar calendar, reminding followers to maintain a vegan diet on the day of the crescent moon and the full moon. They light incense on the altar for their ancestors and place a simple meal of rice, steamed vegetables and soy sauce, along with five different kinds of fruit and yellow flowers, near photographs and paintings of the deceased.

CHAPTER 13

ROUGH WATERS

We had only a few gold ingots left, but I could not let go of the thought of arranging for my family to escape Vietnam. I desperately wanted all of my children to have a brighter future. I asked Phán if I could keep the postcard in my jacket pocket. It became a talisman to maintain my courage and an amulet to guide my decision-making. This time, I would not trust our fate to others.

To execute my new plan, I would need to leave my family behind in Đà Lạt. The night before I left, I could not sleep. I stood beside my children's beds for a long time watching them sleep, trying to capture their images through my tears. All the brothers were in two beds in the same bedroom. All the sisters were in another.

It was raining very hard the morning I left. Was the downpour unusually heavily? I wondered if it was a sign, a warning from Heaven. With a few ingots sewn inside the lining of my coat, I put my small bag across my shoulder, opened the door and left, trying to hold firm to my resolve. Water soaked through my raincoat as I walked quickly to the bus station to begin my journey to the Cà Mau Peninsula, in the southernmost part of Vietnam, an area famous for its fishing, its fish sauce and its mosquitoes. More importantly, many boats were built there every day.

It took two days to travel from Đà Lạt to Cà Mau, and the trip involved several bus rides, boat rides and ferries. When I arrived

I ordered a bowl of noodle soup at a street stall. I noticed an old man ordering one bowl of soup for the young boy he was with and guessed that he did not have enough money to buy one for himself. Through my dark sunglasses, I knew that I could observe them discreetly, without them knowing that I noticed even the small details. The old man ordered the cheapest soup, only noodles and broth, no meat. A few consecutive up and down movements of his thyroid cartilage were visible through the wrinkled skin of his neck. He tried to move his eyes away from the little boy's steaming bowl. The smell of the famous Vietnamese phở filled the entire area.

I turned to him and made my offer. "Allow me to pay for a bowl of phở for you."

The older man looked at me suspiciously.

"I also want to order some meat for your grandson's bowl. I'm guessing he is your grandson. How old is he?"

The little boy stopped eating, looked at me and then at his grandfather.

"Yes, he is my grandson, seven years old."

The lady who owned the stall immediately handed the old man a large bowl, then placed more meat and soup into the little boy's bowl.

I paid for the food immediately to reassure him that I kept my word. We all ate our noodles, savouring the delicious broth.

When he had finished, the old man looked at me kindly. "You are not local, am I correct?"

"You are right. I am from out of town."

"I don't want to intrude, but it seems you have no relatives here. If you want, we can show you around."

He correctly guessed that I knew no one and I felt his suggestion was genuine, but I was still cautious.

"There is only one inn operating so you must be staying there. Be careful of the mosquitoes. Remember, this land is famously described

as *Rừng thiên* (mysterious mountain), *Nước độc* (poisonous water)."
He clearly knew the area well. "If you want, meet me here again
tomorrow morning at about seven, then we can show you around."
He took his grandson's hand and the two of them walked away.

What he said was true. The only inn open was not far from the
phở stall. I checked into a single room for one night, looking forward
to a good night's sleep after two days of travel. As I hung up the mosquito net, securing the corners carefully, I suddenly remembered that
I forgot to ask the old man's name.

The crowing of the rooster announced the start of daily activities
the next morning. I discovered the mosquito net had a few holes
and, as I walked to the phở stall, noticed my arm had a few bites. The
stall was closed so I sat on a bench, lit a cigarette and watched the
locals go about their morning routines, either walking or by bicycle.
Nearby, a communist policeman was patrolling the area; he stopped
at an open food stall to order his breakfast. I stood up to walk away
but caught the sight of the old man and his grandson walking toward
me. I waited for him, then we both walked out of sight of the policeman without saying a word.

"My name is Bảy Thọ. Let's talk at my place. More private."

It was quite a long walk, through streets that eventually led to a
more desolate part of the town. His grandson walked and skipped,
humming a tune. His grandfather joined in, still holding his hand.
For a moment, I wondered if I should trust these strangers. But this
innocent boy and their loving relationship encouraged me to trust
my instinct.

We arrived at their place, a hut located on the side of a dirt road
that led to a mangrove forest. An old canoe was tied to the exposed
root of a huge mangrove tree, and I could see the dark red of a small
altar attached to its trunk. Outside the door, a charred black kettle
sat on a cold stone stove. Another coal-black dented pot was placed

upside down on a pile of sticks. Stepping inside, I noticed the four corner pillars appeared quite solid, but the walls consisted of various sizes of wooden sticks covered with blue tarpaulins. The roof consisted of thick pads of woven palm leaves. A wooden platform that obviously served as the bed occupied most of the area, covering the dirt floor.

The little boy jumped up to the platform and sat on his grandfather's lap, his eyes fixed on me.

"Let me be straightforward. Are you looking for a connection to escape, *vượt biên*?" asked Bảy Thọ.

I remained silent, hesitating.

"Let me guess. Did you just get released from the political re-education camp?" Many ex-prisoners sought ways to escape Vietnam as soon as they were discharged from years of detention.

"I know a reliable source. The organizers asked me to look for people who want to escape. If I find one or two people, the gold they pay will cover the cost for my grandson and me."

I thought Bảy Thọ must be desperate to risk telling me all this.

"My daughter and her family escaped two months ago. I got left behind because the leader, the *để lô*, tricked us. I got separated from the group and the *để lô* disappeared."

I thought of the escape I arranged for Phiên, Phán and Phú, reliving the agony of being deceived and cheated out of my gold. "The *để lô* tricked you? Or was it the organizers of the escape?"

"No, the *để lô*. I know for sure. He was paid to lead me and my grandson. But he cheated. Instead of leading us to where the boat was docked, he left us in a remote spot, then disappeared. The organizers of the escape found out that he replaced us with two of his own escapees, who paid him a substantial amount of gold. The organizers have been looking for him ever since. I hang around this area to see if I can spot him and to wait for news of my family."

I offered him a cigarette. We both stepped outside while his grand-son, Thanh, ran over to the alter and lit the incense. I followed him, lit my own incense and prayed. I offered to buy some rice and canned food plus some candies for Thanh. We walked back to town, had lunch and bought food for dinner.

I had started feeling unwell around midday. By dinner, I felt dizzy and fatigued, with a strange headache. After the meal, I vomited.

"You have a lot of mosquito bites on your arm. I think it is best that you rest here." Bảy Thọ suggested. "It's a long walk back."

I came down with malaria. For two straight days, I slipped in and out of consciousness. Between the bouts of vomiting, I thought of my wife and children waiting for me at home. Bảy Thọ and Thanh fed me warm boiled water.

On the third day, I could sit up and swallow rice soup. I reached for my coat and felt the gold still securely sewn in the lining. I was grateful for Thanh and Bảy Thọ for their kindness.

I thought I could tell him my intentions, but still, I did not want to reveal my full plan. "I want to build a boat, a river boat, to transport goods and produce on the Mekong River, from Cà Mau to Vũng Tàu, a family business."

As soon as I mentioned the river boat, I knew he wouldn't suspect I intended to build a boat to escape. A boat meant for the ocean needed a pointed bow to push through the waves.

"Ah, I see. Then I know a person you should see. My nephew, Bảy Điện, who obtained a permit to build boats in Thốt Nốt. I can write him a note to give you a good deal."

He gave me the address and wrote a letter for me to give to his nephew and I found out that it was not difficult to obtain a permit to build a merchant boat. No one needed to know the true intention behind its construction. It would be one boat among many others, transporting goods along the Mekong River, secretly waiting for the right opportunity. But I realized that to build a boat I would need help from people I could trust.

I took a bus and two ferries to Thốt Nốt to confirm the address. From there I took the bus to Saigon, then travelled home to my wife and my children. As the bus started to climb the plateau to reach Đà Lạt, my heart started to beat faster with a thrill of strange contentment and a curious excitement about this dangerous plan. I again walked home in the pouring rain, but this time my heart was light.

That evening, after a warm and happy meal, my wife and I sat on our bed surrounded by our children. I began by giving them the presents I had brought home, different types of cowrie shells.

Diệu Phương asked, "How do we get to this coast and collect this kind of shell?"

"Where I went, there are plenty of these. Someday we will all travel to this coast to collect them."

Then I showed them my arm, still covered in mosquito bites. I told them about the big mosquitoes, which had tried to suck out all my blood, and how I had conquered the creatures and come home healthy and in one piece. "Where I stayed, the mosquitoes are as big as my thumb. The problem is they come in a group. But now I'm immune to them."

Finally, I told them about my new business venture—I would build a merchant boat to provide for the family. "I will build a boat. It will be our family boat, and we will all travel on it to get to this place so you can freely choose the best shells."

"You'll be a cool captain," said Phổ.

"When can we ride on the boat?" asked Phấn.

The older children were silent. They knew I lied.

I paused for a few seconds and, gathering all my strength, said, "Phú, I think you should be the one who helps me. I have thought extremely hard before I ask you to quit school temporarily to help me with this family business, but this boat will be the gold that saves the livelihood of our family." Of all my children, he resembled me the most and had the strongest character.

"Yes, Father. I am willing to help you," he answered, almost immediately.

I had often told my children that education was the most important tool in building a successful life, and Phú was always at the top of his class. He was almost perfect in every subject and no other student could beat him. Yet here I was, asking him to quit school. At fifteen, it was too much of a burden to place on his young shoulders, but I needed help and I could only place my full trust in an immediate family member.

After a few days visiting at home, I knew we had to leave for Thốt Nốt. Phú and I left Đà Lạt early in the morning, walking through the heavy fog to the bus station in silence, each of us listening to the clamour of our own thoughts. As a father, I was embarrassed that my son, instead of going to school, had to follow me on this perilous path.

We arrived at Thốt Nốt and met Bảy Thợ's nephew, who had received a special permit to build our merchant boat. I left Phú to stay with the family and help with the construction while I went to Saigon and bought an old boat engine we could rebuild. I wanted him to learn everything about the boat and, most important of all, the engine. He needed to know how it worked so he could fix it if there was a problem.

The boat was to be a thirty-six-foot merchant boat equipped with a basic living cabin. Phú and I would travel along the Mekong River transporting sand from Vũng Tàu to Cần Thơ and watermelon from Cần Thơ to Vũng Tàu. The boat would also carry pots, fish sauces and produce to sell at the many ports along this long stretch of river. I wanted Phú to know everything about life on the water and everything about this boat with its rebuilt engine.

It took more than a year to carry out the plan. I left Phú in Thốt Nốt while I travelled to Saigon and Đà Lạt to execute the secret part of the scheme, meeting with small groups of strangers in the middle of the night, whispering in the dark, the steel door tightly shut. I contacted a distant cousin who chose to go by the name of Chú Tư to conceal his identity and avoid complications. He had been the captain of an American ship who, after the fall of Saigon, was immediately arrested and imprisoned. He had just been released from the political re-education camp and wanted to arrange for himself and his two older children to escape Vietnam. He would help Phú navigate the boat while it was at sea. But, to avoid suspicion, he and his children would only arrive on the day of the escape. Slowly, by word of mouth to trusted friends and relatives, I gathered a group of people who wanted to escape and agreed to share the cost of running this pretend business.

Boat merchants were never able to make a profit because the communist government set up boat inspection stations at every port along the Mekong River. Every time a boat passed through an inspection station, the boat owner had to pay a "merchant boat fee." It was just another scheme to satisfy their greed but, subsidized by our partners, the boat improved our circumstances. My wife was able to join me, leaving Phiên and Hằng Phương in charge of the household. Phiên was in his last year at teacher college and Hằng Phương was entering her second year of college, studying to become a nurse. Phán had passed the university exam and now attended the University of Economics in Saigon. One of his main tasks was to visit Đà Lạt to check on his siblings and to bring sugar, dried squid, rice and other foods unavailable there. Whenever he had free time, he helped Phú with operating the boat.

My wife and I visited home whenever we could. Our children reassured us that they were old enough to take care of themselves. Phiên was a gentle person who never enforced any strict rules and Hằng Phương cooked delicious meals. Phi became the family chess champion, and Phi, Phổ and Phấn often took first place in their classes. Lan Phương and Diệu Phương continued to be inseparable.

I taught Phú to master the business. We took a pretend fishing trip to test the boat in the ocean. I trained him to navigate skillfully through rough water. He would be a second captain when this boat embarked on its perilous escape. We endured every fierce inspection from the communist officials. We had to bribe them and put up with constant harassment, but we survived each day, burying our anger and anxiety, keeping our focus on the priceless freedom awaiting us across the Pacific Ocean.

CHAPTER 14

TRẠI MÁT

Two days before I left Đà Lạt, I arranged a short trip to visit Trại Mát, the village about seven kilometres away where my parents operated their pharmacy from 1971 to 1975. I left the hotel before dawn, when the usual fog was making its misty formations on the ground, so that I could catch the sunrise on the clouds floating among the lustrous greens of the mountain.

The pharmacy had been custom built with living quarters at the back where we could stay overnight. A few steps from the back of the building, there was a barn where we raised chickens and pigs. The farm was a few kilometres away. That was where, during most of our summers, Father taught us to plant and harvest the corn, beans and sweet potatoes that often added to our daily meals. In the evening, Father would roast corn cobs on an open fire until the husk charred, a delicious late-night snack. I was picky and did not want to eat right from the cob, so Father picked kernels off the cob to feed me. Whenever I eat corn, I recall this loving gesture.

In addition to Mother's work as a nurse, the pharmacy functioned as a clinic, treating minor injuries. Everyone in the village visited the pharmacy to buy medicine and seek treatment for illnesses ranging from a common cold to severe fever. One time, Father rushed in carrying a boy whose chin had been severely cut. Father comforted him while Mother tended to his wound. Later, we helped clean the blood off the cement floor and washed our parents' bloody clothes.

We often helped watch the pharmacy while our parents tended to patients in their homes but were never allowed to leave the proximity of the pharmacy or the barn. The thick pine forests, abundant with waterfalls that formed natural streams, were ideal hiding places for Viet Cong, so the American army had planted landmines in many of the fields. Once in a while an explosion would shake the entire village. Seconds later, the tranquil town would transform into chaos with people running, screaming and crying. Crowds would gather in front of the pharmacy to watch Mother and Father treat the injured. Father once used his Jeep Cherokee to drive a boy who lost one of his legs to the hospital. He had ventured onto the grass while tending his water buffalo, bloody pieces of which now littered the field. Afterward, "one-leg boy" often came to the barn to sell hay to Father, who paid him more than the real value of his products. The villagers respectfully addressed Father and Mother as *Ông Bà Thuốc Tây*, the Medicine Couple.

More than thirty years later, I stood looking at the run-down building, wholly shut, with no sign of any occupants. The barn was empty too, devoid of any indication of living animals. The building next door was a ruin, its broken bricks and wrecked walls adding to the desolation. I felt the pain in my heart, fully comprehending my parents' torment. The wealth they had lost couldn't compare to the loss of their careers and their dedication to the life of this town.

The year that Lan Phương turned three, she came down with a high fever. My older brothers and sister were still at school and Father was out of town so Phú and I took care of her.

I was holding my sister carefully in my arms. "We must let Mother know," I said to Phú, feeling the heat transmitted by Lan Phương's feverish body.

"She is somewhere in Trại Mát, but I don't know where exactly," said Phú in a worried voice, his eyes on the clock. "I could take the bicycle to look for her, but by the time I get there, she will probably be on the bus home." At that moment, we realized that we never knew where she went each day. The pharmacy had been confiscated and the building was now occupied by some communist officials.

I shifted my arms and Lan Phương cried. I cried along with her.

"Let me hold her for you. You are scaring her with your tears."

"You have to hold her very still, like a statue, or she will feel the movement and cry again," I said, still sobbing. I was praying to the earth spirits, whose anger we were told caused illness, to let me endure her fever instead. I thought of what Grandmother said about respecting the spirits and wanted to explain to them that my youngest sister had done nothing wrong.

Lan Phương stopped screaming and fell asleep while Phú held her very still, his skinny arms frozen into position. I knew he was even more worried than me but was trying to be calm for both his younger sisters.

Our three younger brothers, Phi, Phổ and Phấn stood by the door, anxiously watching for the first sight of Mother. Time passed more slowly than usual; the air heavy with an unnerving silence intended to keep Lan Phương from waking up.

"Mother is home. Mother is home at last!" Phi, Phổ and Phấn screamed at the same time, startled Lan Phương, who instantly began to cry. Mother was finally home from her exhausting day with groceries to cook supper. We all cried in panic as she hurried inside the house, putting her hand on Lan Phương's forehead. Her face turned pale and, just for a moment, her expression was horrified.

"She is too warm. When did it start?"

"Around noon, so about five hours ago. We did not know where you were. We did not know what to do," Phú told Mother, trying to keep his voice calm.

"I want you to fetch me some cold water now," Mother told Phú. Then she turned to me. "Jolie, stop crying." Her voice was loud. "You have an important task. Listen to me very carefully."

She put both her hands on my shoulders, looked straight into my eyes, and lowered her voice. "You need to run to this address." Mother whispered it into my ear along with instructions on how to get there. Something about a street named Tân Văn Danh.

"Now, Jolie, memorize this address. Repeat it back to me," said Mother firmly.

I couldn't remember a word she said. I looked at her, wiping my tears, my mind blank.

"Let me do it, Mother" said Phú, "Jolie can't stop crying. She is still shaking. Let me do it."

Mother ignored him. She did not want to waste time explaining.

"One of you get Jolie the thick raincoat," Mother told my younger brothers. All three ran to get it.

Mother sat me down and put the raincoat on me. "Jolie, calm down, listen to me. Only you can do this important task. I don't have time to explain." She tore a piece of paper, wrote "6T," then rolled the note around some paper money. She placed it securely in the inner pocket of the raincoat then wrote the address onto my palm. She pressed hard but I was numb to the pain.

Mother again put her arms on my shoulders to reassure me. "Jolie, you can do this. Run as fast as you can to this address. You will know when you get there. Just ask for the mother of this household and give her what I put in the pocket. Tell her your sister has a high fever. Your sister will get better with what you will bring back."

As I was about to run out of the door, Mother stopped me. "Wait!

Jolie, if anyone stops you, you must spit into your palm, and scrub your hands together to erase the address." She gave me another reassuring nod. "Now, go quickly. Jolie, you can do it!"

I took the shortcut through the temple compound behind the house. I realized I knew this street; it was near the school. I ran as fast as I could, catching my breath along the way, and arrived at the address. To my surprise, I recognized the house of my classmate. We were good friends and often did homework together at her home. I knew the house but had never noticed the address.

I peered through the glass of the front door, looking for a glimpse of my friend. Then I remembered she often told me to look for her at the back door, where the kitchen was, so I went straight to the back of the house.

She was surprised to see me. "Diệu Phương, why are you here? I didn't think we agreed to do homework together tonight. Don't come in. It is very stinky. I am washing my baby brother's dirty sheets."

I ignored her and stepped inside, holding my nose. "I must see your mother. My mother sent me."

My friend's mother came into the room and, sensing the urgency, immediately took me to her bedroom. "Your mother sent you? Did she send a note?" she asked in a lowered voice.

I gave her a quick bow before I answered her. "Yes, my sister has a high fever right now. My mother sent you this." I took the rolled note out from the pocket of the giant raincoat.

She unrolled the note, put the money in her pocket and asked me to wait in the room. She quickly returned with six pills of Tylenol carefully wrapped in layers of brown paper. She secured the little parcel inside the pocket of my raincoat.

"Be careful running back, but before you leave, let's go to the kitchen." She took me to the sink and washed the address off my palm.

I ran back home, feeling the pocket with the drugs that would save my youngest sister. Now I understood why I had to wear this rain-coat—the pocket was gigantic, keeping this precious and illegal drug secure and, if the rain came, it would not get wet.

Phú greeted me at the door. "Good job, Jolie, I know why Mother sent you on this dangerous task." Hằng Phương, Phán and Phiên were back from school and I smelled the familiar scent of cooked rice, ready for supper.

Mother immediately cut the pill in half, ground it to a powder and mixed it with warm rice broth to spoon-feed Lan Phương, reassuring us that she would be fine. Mother said the Tylenol would make her feel much better. That night, we all took turns sitting beside Lan Phương, gently putting our hands on her forehead to feel her body temperature.

Mother complimented my effort at the dinner table that evening. Her first choice would have been to keep what she did a secret, but she had run out of Tylenol that day and needed her black-market trading partner. My friend and I now knew each other's secret, but we never mentioned it again. A tiny hint or an accidental leak could lead to our families being convicted with a high possibility of being sent to the new economic zone.

Mother stayed up that whole night to take care of Lan Phương. I heard her cursing while grinding the Tylenol in the middle of the night, thinking her children were all asleep. A nurse who used to own a pharmacy found herself without any medication to treat her feverish daughter.

The next day, Father came back from his trip and we learned that he travelled to different cities to buy medicines from well-hidden black markets. Every time I looked up to the ceiling hiding place in the kitchen, I could not help but recall the bright, elegant pharmacy that my parents used to own, now shrunk into a damp, dark and clandestine space.

Three days later, Lan Phương was much better, although a red rash broke out on her skin. Mother said she had measles but had passed the dangerous point of the illness. We had all been vaccinated when we were young but Lan Phương, who was born under the communist regime, had had to fight for her immunity.

Phú celebrated by putting Lan Phương on the bicycle. Her little hands held tightly to the handlebars and her eyes sparkled in the sunshine as we pushed her around the cement front yard. She was laughing out loud as the breeze blew her ebony hair across her face. My heart held on to that moment because, only a few years later, she would only exist in memory.

Whenever Father was not home, Mother continued to drag herself to Trại Mát every day, resenting her daily work more than ever. The village that once marked the peak of her career now signified rock bottom. It was a bitterness she had to force herself to confront every day, as it was the only way she could put food on the table for us. When she returned, she often withdrew to bed where she would moan softly, reminding me of the Triton shell Father had given me. She too had become an empty shell whose hollowness made a mournful sound, only returning to her old self when Father came home. I occasionally received packages through her usual contacts; with no strength left, Mother would ask me to hide or retrieve medicines from the ceiling above the kitchen.

CHAPTER 15

VượT BIÊN

I finally decided on the escape day: May 19, 1983, Hồ Chí Minh's birthday and a national holiday. May was also the month in which the wind and the Pacific Ocean would be considerately calm. The boat would be anchored near Vũng Tàu, close to where the Mekong River meets the Pacific Ocean. Phú would stay with the boat, on guard against any surprise inspections from communist officials. But staffing levels would be reduced and the chances that those on duty would neglect their responsibilities in favour of the celebrations were high. The escapees had been divided into small groups, each with a *đề lô* who would direct them to either a canoe or water taxi, the most convenient method of transportation along the narrow and shallow waterways of the Mekong River.

Mỹ Phương and her young family would stay behind and live in our home in Đà Lạt. I arranged for my wife and my eight other children to stay in three adjoining rooms at a hotel in Saigon, bringing them there in small groups. Ironically, this period felt a bit like a vacation, a short reprieve, a strange calmness before an unpredictable storm. For the first time in many years, the children had no chores to do, no homework, no cooking or cleaning. While they waited for everyone to assemble, they were free to spend time with each other, telling stories, playing games and trying not to think about their murky future.

My wife and I tried to act normal, doing our best to hide the stress of making a monumental decision. I had become obsessed by the fear that my entire family could be imprisoned, with no one left to find the correct officials to bribe. Mỹ Phương would not be capable of dealing with the evils of the system and I would not want her to bear this immense responsibility. If my plan succeeded, we could all be free. But if it failed, the disaster would be complete. I thought often of the family that had committed suicide. We finally decided that only my six older children and Phiên's fiancée, Thu Hà, would escape. We would entrust their care to Chú Tư and stay behind with the three youngest children.

Two nights before the escape, May 17, we went to a restaurant for dinner. We knew this would be the last opportunity to be together for a long time and encouraged everyone to order anything they wanted. The children ordered their favourite fish among other dishes. As the boat owner, we were careful to follow the tradition of not flipping the fish over so that no bad luck would come to the boat. When the fried kingfish arrived, we carefully removed the bones before passing the dish to the children, a habit that my wife and I acquired through years of worrying the fish bones would be stuck in their little throats. Our children were getting older, and this was likely no longer necessary, but it was a traditional, loving gesture that we wanted to make to our children before parting from them.

I noticed a half-Western, half-Vietnamese boy sitting on the floor in a corner. He had been here the last time we visited this restaurant; my wife told me he had snatched my bowl from the table as soon as I went outside to smoke. This time, I asked the waiter for an extra big bowl, filled it with a bit of all the dishes we ordered and took it over to him. He sat still for a few seconds as I put the bowl in his hands, then began to eat so quickly I was afraid he would choke.

When we returned to the hotel, I called a meeting with Phiên, Thu

Hà, Hằng Phương, Phán, Diệu Phương and Phi. As arranged, my wife kept the younger children busy in another room. I started by giving each of them a thick roll of bills secured by an elastic band. "Keep this cash safe. You may have to use it. Now, listen to me carefully. Tomorrow afternoon, I will take you to the bus to Vũng Tàu. We will meet a man wearing a black hat. This man is called *đề lô*. He will ask me a secret question. I will reply with the matching answer to confirm he is the correct person to lead you to a safe house. From there, he will give you further instructions. I will signal you to get on the bus with this man. Do not talk to him or ask any questions. Before he signals the bus driver to stop the bus so he can get off, he will take his hat off and wipe his forehead. He will keep his hat off until you all notice. Watch out for that signal, then prepare to get off the bus as well. After that, just follow him. Make sure to keep a good distance behind and avoid drawing attention to yourselves."

I paused to make sure everyone understood, then made my voice even more serious. "In case our plans fail and you get caught, there are important procedures that I need each one of you to remember."

I could tell by their expressions that they were beginning to understand I would no longer be coming with them. "I will pair you up and give you fake names. You must try to hide your real names altogether. Try not to give them any hints that you are brothers and sisters. If you get caught, then remember what I am about to tell you next and stick to your story. That will buy me time to bail you out."

I tried to lighten my voice, using a bit of humour to ease the tension. I turned to Hằng Phương. "You and Jolie stay together as sisters. Your fake name will be Nguyễn Thị Đẹp (Đẹp means beautiful). This name should be easy to remember because your Mother thinks you are the prettiest. Jolie, your fake name will be Nguyễn Thị Hồng because this hot weather makes your cheeks turn pink (Hồng means pink)."

I saw Diệu Phương's raise her eyebrows slightly; pink was not her favourite colour. But my wife thought that name would make her notice and remember, and I agreed with her idea. She worried that Diệu Phương's mind was often in some obscure clouds.

Phi started giggling when he heard the fake names for his two older sisters. Phán tried not to laugh and signalled Phi to concentrate.

I tried to sound serious. "You both have the last name Nguyễn because you are sisters. Stay together and if anyone asks about your background just say that you both lived in the countryside and came to Saigon to sell cigarettes on the street. Never reveal your home address."

I turned to Phi and Phán and noticed Phi was still stifling a laugh. Phán's hand covered his mouth as he tried to remain serious. "Phi and Phán, you stay together. You both claim to be brothers. Phán, your nickname is Bert, so your fake name will be Lê Be. Phi, your nickname is Robert, so your fake name is Lê Rô. Again, never reveal the location of this hotel or where you live. Just say you came to Saigon to make a living selling cigarettes on the street."

Everyone started laughing, partly at the names and partly to relieve the tension. I joined in but felt the stress of this fateful decision taking its toll on me. Afraid they were missing the fun, the younger children ran in to join us. My wife followed and looked at me wordlessly. Then she took Hằng Phương aside to tell her she had sewn small pieces of gold into the lining of her undershirt.

I asked Phiên and Phán to join me in another room to give them private instructions. "Phiên, you can think of fake names for you and your fiancée. You can agree on what story you both want, as long as it is consistent. Your mother and I have hidden medicine for motion sickness behind the altar in the cabin. The hold is currently filled with clay pots that contain water and dried rice. More than half of them are empty. The top two layers are the empty ones; they conceal the water and the food supplies for the voyage. Once you get on to the boat, instruct some men to throw the empty pots into the river to make room for the passengers. Phú might be busy checking the passenger list."

At dawn, May 18, I rented a bicycle from the hotel and rode to the port to inform Phú of the change of plan. My heart sank, seeing his tanned, skinny figure standing on the boat. I stopped to wipe away the tears behind my dark sunglasses, hoping he hadn't seen me. It took all my strength to climb the steps to the boat. I hesitated for a moment and then told him my decision. He didn't say much as tears flowed down his cheeks. I knew he wanted to object, but Phú remained silent, keeping his thoughts to himself. After almost three years of working alongside each other, we were forced to confront a farewell we had not anticipated. I hugged him tightly and kissed his forehead.

Finally, I reminded him to remember all my instructions. After years of careful observation, I had identified and paid all the correct officials to stay away from the area and arranged for the Coast Guard to turn a blind eye. Once all family members were on board, Phú would raise the anchor, then strip off the license plate, tie it to a rock, and throw it into the river to destroy the boat's identity. After we parted, I rode the bicycle as Phú drove the boat along the shore. He watched me and I watched him until we each faded from sight.

On the way back to the hotel, I stopped and bought rare and expensive Vietnamese sausage—the kind that was offered at the ancestral altar, then served with sticky rice during Tết, the Lunar New Year—and delicious jasmine rice to take back to my family for lunch. It had been a long time since we had tasted this mixture of salty and sweet flavours.

After lunch, I gave each of the older children a brown bag full of dried sugar mixed with lime. During a visit to the boat, Lan Phương had helped Phú and me squeeze limes into white sugar, spread the mixture on a sheet and dry it under the sun until it could be broken into chunks. "Keep these bags with you. While at sea, pieces can be dissolved in water to make lime juice that will help fight thirst. If you take a piece and let it melt in your mouth it will help ease seasickness."

Without a word, they followed me out of the hotel. I walked my bicycle a short distance ahead of them until we arrived at an alley, a deserted, dirty corner near the bus station. I lit a cigarette and leaned against a dilapidated wall, not looking at my children and trying to blend in with the crowds, until a mid-sized bus pulled into the alley and stopped a few metres away. The man with the black hat stepped out of the vehicle and we exchanged the codes. Then the moment had come—I signalled my family to follow the man onto the bus and smiled a silent farewell. As the engine started and the dust began to swirl, I waved a discreet goodbye and then followed on the bicycle as far as I could. When I could no longer keep up, I stood on the side of the road and watched the bus recede into the distance.

CHAPTER 16
THE ĐỂ LÔ

We boarded the bus under the curious gaze of the other passengers and sat on two facing benches each other, making it hard to avoid cautious eye contact. They appeared to be locals taking this bus to Vũng Tàu. I recalled Mother telling me our skin was fairer than that of the people who lived in this region, so I'm sure we stood out. The *để lô* with the black hat sat quietly at the end of the opposite bench.

It was a long and rough ride. After more than two hours of being bounced around by potholes, the bus reached Bà Rịa, Vũng Tàu. The *để lô* took his hat off and wiped his forehead, giving us the signal that we should prepare to get off.

We followed him through narrow and dirty roads, where the houses shared walls and the ground was covered with garbage from the busy street stalls. I remembered Father's words and tried to look straight ahead. The locals glanced at us then ignored us; it appeared they were used to seeing strangers walk through their town.

It was still daytime when we reached an open field with small houses farther apart and a huge poultry barn in the distance. The air was thick with the smell of chicken manure. The *để lô* led us to a house connected to the poultry barn and knocked on the door, his knuckles rapping a code. An older woman answered and immediately led us to the back of the house, where the chickens were kept.

She pointed to a wooden platform about half a metre above the ground, told us to settle on it and left. The chickens and roosters flew away from us, making unpleasant squawking noises to protest the humans who had invaded their living space.

My head hurt from the humidity mixed with the putrid smell of animal waste. I lay down on the platform and used a shirt to cover my nose, wondering if the woman thought that chickens and roosters did not need fresh air. How could they survive in such gloomy and smelly conditions, living in their own feces? The barn was dark, with only a small window at the top corner through which no light shone; night had fallen.

After a few hours, the chickens and the roosters seemed to get used to us and started to venture near our platform. Some tried to fly up; we had to make them fly back down. They clucked angrily at us. The woman came back to the barn, carrying an oil lamp, and introduced herself as Bà Mười Thiếu. Perhaps she had heard the loud racket the birds were making.

"How long do we have to stay here?" Phiên asked her.

"For some reason, I received word that you need to have another để lô. I have to wait for that person to come and give me the correct codes before I can let you all go with him," she replied with a southern, Saigon accent. "If you want to have something to eat, I cooked you a meal, but you have to pay me."

Hằng Phương answered. "I think we should have some dinner. We do not know how long we will have to wait."

Bà Mười Thiếu collected the money from Phiên and left. I wondered if anyone could eat in this environment. My head hurt even more.

It turned out that we could eat in her kitchen, which was connected to the barn by a small, confined yard. Earlier in the afternoon, when I had walked to this house, I'd been disgusted by the foul air, but now it was a vast improvement over the inside of the barn. How could people breathe this in their whole life?

There was no electricity. We sat down on a bench and ate the simple meal she had cooked for us: a bowl of rice with some fried eggs and squash soup. I ate slowly, hoping to delay returning to the barn.

We were still in the house when the intermittent crowing of the roosters indicated that it was midnight. Shortly after, we heard three knocks on the door, a pause, two knocks, another pause, then one last knock. Bà Mười Thiểu placed her ear on the door to hear the whispered voice of a man.

"Bà Mười Thiểu, I am here to pick up the rice and six chicken eggs."

Bà Mười Thiểu opened the door. I wondered if the six chicken eggs referred to the six of us. Another man in another black hat walked into the room. He was the second để lô, the one who would take us to our boat. He stood silently and observed all of us for a few seconds. He turned to Bà Mười Thiểu, murmured something, then turned around, walked quickly to the door and left.

"He says the shirt of your sister is too bright. The blue and the white will glow in the dark," Bà Mười Thiểu said to Phiên, looking at me. "He said the glow of her shirt may jeopardize the entire group while you are walking through the village to get to the fen. She must change to a shirt with a darker colour." Bà Mười Thiểu kept her eyes on me.

"I don't have a dark coloured shirt. The other one is white." I replied, wondering why I did not know of this ahead of time. "Do you have a dark colour shirt that I could buy from you? It does not matter if it is old or a rag. I want to wear it over this shirt." I was pleased to have thought of this solution so quickly, but I was very aware she could set any price she wanted to for one old shirt.

She nodded her head, went to another room and returned with a traditional dark grey *áo bà ba,* the old-fashioned blouse worn by middle-aged southern Vietnamese women. I had never worn a top like this but pulled it on over my blue and white shirt.

"I don't want to take any money for this old blouse. I want to exchange it for the other white shirt, the one you held to your nose earlier."

That shirt was the one Father had helped me chose at my aunt's fabric shop, the one with the pattern of tiny mushrooms. It was precious to me, not just because it was pretty but because it reminded me of the special time that I had spent with him.

"I want to give that shirt to my granddaughter. She is as skinny as you, and you don't need it anymore." She was trying to convince me.

Why would she say that I wouldn't need that shirt anymore? Was she hinting that I would die on the trip? Should I contradict her? But Father had taught me that if there was nothing good to say, it was best to stay quiet. I held out some bills to pay for the old *áo bà ba.*

"You don't have a lot of time left. The other *đế lô* is coming back soon." Bà Mười Thiều insisted, pushing the money away.

Everyone was looking at me, waiting for me to give this woman the shirt. Even though I knew that this woman was crucial to the next phase of the escape, I wavered. She said that other man was the *đế lô,* but he had left. We could not trust her, but we could not afford to anger her either. She held the secret codes, and we were not sure when that *đế lô* would be back. I reluctantly handed her my favourite shirt.

Taking it, she ordered us back to the barn to wait. I worried about how long I could survive breathing that foul air if anything went wrong. The roosters gave another long crow: one hour past midnight.

To my relief, the door swung open soon after. The dim light shining through the dirty glass of the oil lamp briefly showed the faces of the *đế lô* and Bà Mười Thiều. He led us through the fields until we reached another village with small houses crowded around a narrow alley. We walked on dirt paths barely illuminated by the dim light of a few windows.

Suddenly, another group crossed our path. The *đề lô* stopped walking and gestured for us to stand still. I almost bumped into Hằng Phương, who was ahead of me. I grabbed her back. Someone in the other group fell to the ground. Some kids started crying, then a dog started to bark; all the other village dogs joined in. Villagers turned on lights in their homes, and a woman emerged from a cottage, shrieking "*Vượt biên! Vượt biên!*"

The light shining through the window of the house beside us revealed another path. The *đề lô* made a right turn and ran. We ran after him, trying to get away from the strangers in the other group. He led us down an empty road, then suddenly veered off the road and ducked under a weeping willow tree whose branches reached the ground. We followed him and hid. The chaotic noise of barking dogs, running feet and panting searchers reached us as we crouched behind the curtain of greenery. The squealing voice of the woman who had yelled *vượt biên* echoed in the distance; it seemed like we were some distance out of the village.

Without a word, the *đề lô* disappeared into the night, leaving us to our confusion and fear.

"I think we are going to get caught," said Hằng Phương gloomily, "the *đề lô* has run away already!"

"We should just wait here for now, to see what is going on. I think he will be back." Phiên tried to calm us down.

"I don't think he will leave us here. Phú will not drive the boat anywhere if he does not see us getting on board." Phán reassured us, his voice calm. "Father told me that the *đề lô* got paid extra to lead us to the boat because we are the children of the owner. Without us, Phú will turn back."

"Oh no! Fire ants! They're crawling on my feet. Jolie, get away from this spot!" Hằng Phương jumped away, hammering her feet on the ground while trying to keep her voice low.

I jumped up and hit my head on a branch. Luckily, I was wearing my blue hat and the brim partially protected my face from being scratched. Phi broke the branch to make space for me. Hằng Phương seemed to be fine, having brushed the biting insects away. We noticed the noise from the village had stopped. The silence became tense as we waited under the tree. The willow's branches moved back and forth in the breeze, as if mourning our decision to escape. I tried to look at my watch to read the time, but it was too dark. It seemed to me we had been waiting for at least an hour.

I looked up to a sky full of stars, very different from the perpetual cloud cover of Đà Lạt. I found the seven stars of the Big Dipper and traced up the two pointer stars at the front edge of its cup to find Polaris. I had heard that many lost travellers looked for Polaris to guide them in the right direction and wished I could fly into that open space to find my way out of this predicament. Then I saw a shooting star. I wanted to yell out to my brothers and sister to look at this rare phenomenon and make a wish, but remembered I had to keep quiet. I made a wordless wish of my own.

"I hear some noises. The shadows seem to be moving and I think I see flickering lights. I think people are walking toward us!" Phán broke the silence.

The sound of footsteps was getting louder, the outlines of moving people clearer. Everyone was wearing dark clothing and carrying small bags just like us. The *dẫ lô* emerged from among them and made his way into our hiding spot. "Come out, join this group and follow them."

He led the way and the people started to run ahead of us. We were running to keep up without knowing the exact direction we were heading. Soon we entered muddy grasslands near a waterway that connected with the Mekong River. The ground was slimy and slippery and sucked at my feet. I did not want to lose my only pair of flip-flops so I took them off and slid one over each wrist. I continued to run beside my brothers, holding hands with Hằng Phương.

The night was turning into dawn by the time we reached the edge of the waterway. Murky water came up to our knees. We joined another group of about thirty women, children and men who had arrived before us. The canoes and the water taxis were waiting to take the escapees to the boat, which was anchored in deeper water about ten metres away. Children were crying while women and men yelled at the boat operators to hurry up and paddle to where they stood. I saw Phú emerge from the cockpit, looking for us in the crowd.

"Where are the children of the boat owner?" A man on a water taxi yelled.

"Here!" yelled Phiên and Phán at the same time.

"We are bringing the compass, map and equipment to navigate the boat," two women beside us yelled. One of them was holding a baby boy.

"Children of the boat owner go first. The big boat will not move an inch without them. Let them through! Hurry!" Our second đề lô jumped off a water taxi and pushed it further inland to where we stood. We got on with the two women and the baby.

"Women and children move to the other two water taxis," the driver shouted. He used his paddles to push away the men who fought to get on.

The đề lô paddled toward the escape boat, where I saw Phú was holding a line, anxiously awaiting our arrival. Phiên and Phán quickly climbed up to the deck and helped the rest of us. I was too short to reach the stanchion and struggled to clamber onto the deck while people around me pushed and screamed. I panicked amid the chaos.

"Jolie, try harder! You can do it." Phán shouted, pushing others away to try to catch my hand.

I still could not pull myself up. Phú appeared beside Phán, and both reached down to grab my wrists and lift me to the deck. My siblings and I settled in the cabin near the cockpit, along with other escapees.

Outside, the chaos and screaming continued. Many people filled the hold, removing the clay pots to make room. Phiên and Phán stood on the deck, picking up the pots that emerged from the hold and throwing them into water. Two men at the bow did the same thing. The sounds of the pots hitting the water, the roar of the boat engine, the men shouting, the women screaming and the children crying filled the air and echoed across the land in what was now broad daylight.

People were still running across the muddy field to try to get to the boat. Some men jumped into the shallow water and swam toward us. They got on the boat from the bow and quickly made their way to the hold. Others pushed the *đề lô* into the water and started paddling the water taxi toward us.

Phú was holding a paper that looked like a passenger list. He looked around to check, then called out to a man who appeared to be his assistant to pull the anchor. Then he turned the wheel to drive the boat away. The engine reverberated, struggling to adjust to the weight of its human cargo. Phú tried to steer the boat away from the people who were swimming toward us. They screamed and cursed, threatening to report the escape to the authorities until they were left far behind.

While looking straight ahead, Phú said to Phán, "There are many more people on our boat than anticipated. We do not know these people. They are not the ones on the list."

"We got held up back at the village because a woman started screaming *vượt biên, vượt biên.* Everybody scattered and the *đề lô* left us for hours before coming back to lead us to the fen. There were many people following us." Phán replied.

"Her shout was weird. That woman who screamed didn't sound surprised, just cruel," Phiên added.

Father's cousin, who we addressed as Chú Tư, joined us. He was supposed to be the first captain and only Phú had met him before. Chú Tư was in his early fifties, but his hair was completely white; the hardship from seven years spent in the political re-education camp made him look older than he was. He appeared calm and explained, "Those people might be villagers who knew about the escape. Your father bribed the local police to avoid patrolling the area. Perhaps the local police also took gold from those people and leaked the location to them."

Chú Tư paused. "The đễ lô could also be to blame. The scream could have been a setup to put more fear into vulnerable escapees so that he could divert them to a different path and lose them intentionally. Then his own people, who paid him directly, could take their place on the boat."

"The đễ lô came back to find us, after he left us at the willow tree for hours," said Phán.

Phiên concluded, "He probably realized that we are the boat owner's children, and knew that the boat would not depart without us."

"That explains the delay," said Phú. "The boat was supposed to depart at night, as Father had instructed, not in broad daylight." Now he had the answer to the question he had asked Phiên and Phán as soon as they boarded.

Chú Tư spread out the seaway map and used a ruler to sketch the coordinates. "We would have needed more aggressive measures to prevent these new passengers from invading our boat. And I do not think any of you could do that."

Phú handed the wheel to Chú Tư. "I think it is the time to destroy the license plate. We have about seven kilometres until we reach the ocean."

Phú had taken off the license plate earlier. Now he tied it onto a rock and placed it in a black plastic bag. He walked to the stern, stood for a few seconds and threw the bag into the river.

He came back to the wheel. "It is not over yet. We still have to pass the inspection station near the mouth of the river. The people below need to be quiet and invisible."

Chú Tư yelled at the people in the hold to stay quiet. A woman screamed as two men closed the door by the bow.

Then he warned everyone. "The next hours are very critical. As we pass the station, you must remain absolutely silent. We must pray that we do not encounter any Coast Guards who patrol the area where this river meets the Pacific Ocean."

Under the bright sunlight, the boat ran smoothly on the remaining segment of the Mekong River. Near the mouth of the river, where the murky water started to change its hue, Phú turned off the engine and let the boat glide past the main inspection boathouse. Our prayers were as silent as the boat moving with the river's flow, and there was no sign of any aggressive inspectors with the guns across their shoulders. Just as Father predicted, they were probably still intoxicated from the night before. When the station was far behind, Phú restarted the engine and sped into the Pacific Ocean.

I lay down in the corner of the cabin, resting my aching head on my blue Puma bag, exhausted from a sleepless night. The smell of the chicken barn still lingered, and my pants were covered with dried mud. I started to feel nauseated and reached into my bag for a small lump of the lime and sugar mixture. But my stomach was still trying to push something up my throat. I did not want to throw up in such a small and confined space so I dragged myself toward the stern. Hằng Phương followed to help me.

I knelt down, holding on to the rail, and vomited into the ocean, my stomach expelling the rice, fried eggs and soup. The wind blew away the smell and the propeller sprayed my face with tiny droplets. Looking down at the seawater moving against the hull, I felt dizzy, as though the boat was tilting to the side. I dragged myself back to my spot in the cabin, Hằng Phương right behind me, and lay down, relieved to feel sleepy. I wished I could fall into a deep sleep and have someone wake me when it was all over.

CHAPTER 17

WHAT IF

What had I done? As soon as the bus pulled away, I began to question myself. Why had I put my children in such peril? I could have sent them to their deaths. They could vanish in the ocean and I would never know. What kind of father was not there to protect his children? I was disgusted with myself and overwhelmed by guilt. My imagination tortured me.

What if they were attacked by Thai pirates? They were known to be murderous and evil. I had instructed Phú to avoid the ocean near the Gulf of Thailand so many times. Did they take that route?

What if the engine stopped, and he could not fix it? I had equipped the boat with a spare engine, but still . . .

What if the food ran out? I had packed the boat with rice, dried squid, dried fish—more than a month's supply—but what if it wasn't enough?

What if the water ran out? There was a huge tank of fresh water and I had even packed lime juice. But who knew how long it would have to last?

What if they got lost? I had equipped the boat with a navy compass.

What if they ran out of fuel? They had enough fuel to reach Singapore.

What if a storm sank the boat? I had checked the weather forecast numerous times. May should be the ideal month.

My head echoed with what if . . . what if . . .

My mind was dark with negative and weary thoughts.

I was devastated and exhausted both mentally and physically, but I still had a family who needed me. I returned to the hotel and tried to behave normally, both to reassure the children and to avoid raising suspicion. We left the hotel and returned to Đà Lạt in virtual silence, wordlessly preparing ourselves for the anticipated ongoing petty harassment from the communist officials.

CHAPTER 18

THE BODHISATTVA OF COMPASSION

The boat exited the mouth of the Mekong River around noon. The sky was clear, with only a few scattered clouds. The sun sparkled on a calm Pacific Ocean. At the shoreline, the trees and the mountain receded to a green line edging the ocean. Ahead of us, the sea met the blue sky, a limitless horizon we hoped meant freedom.

Phiên and Phán began distributing water to the passengers, and did a head count: sixty-six people, twice the anticipated capacity. Many men we did not know had slipped aboard amid the chaos. None of us was aggressive enough to force them off the boat even though I sensed that a few of these men had given Phú some trouble earlier.

My headache lingered and sleep eluded me. Hằng Phương gave me a pill to help with nausea, taken from the supply Mother and Father had hidden in a crack behind the cabin's altar in preparation for the journey.

I heard some panicked noises from the hold. Phú informed Chú Tư that another ship was following ours. The engine roared louder than usual as we accelerated—we were not yet in international waters. A Vietnamese patrol ship spotted us and headed in our direction. Phú pushed the throttle to its maximum as people became more anxious. I heard a loud bang as the patrol boat fired a warning shot. Phú cut the engine, suddenly stalling the boat in the middle of the sea.

People in the hold started to scream. Men began to curse, declaring that we had been caught, that we were about to rot in a communist prison. Women cried, and some started to pray. I almost choked, the pill that Hằng Phương had given me stuck in my throat.

The patrol boat stopped beside us, the flag of communist Vietnam, a yellow star centred on a red rectangular, fluttering on top of its big cabin. Men in civilian clothes with guns stood on the deck; some jumped to ours and back threw a line, tying our boat to theirs. Within a few seconds, armed officers stood beside Phú, Phiên and Phán. Another man jumped onto the deck and pointed a gun through the door to the hold. People cried out. Some knelt and began kowtowing to the policemen.

"Who is the boat owner? Where is he?" One officer shouted, waving his gun and striking fear into everyone. Some passengers immediately pointed to Phú, then pointed out the rest of the Hoàng brothers and sisters.

"The boat owner is not on the boat. Those are the boat owner's children," one passenger in the hold yelled, his finger pointed straight at my brothers. We were all horrified, but they were brave and appeared calm, perhaps remembering Father's instructions to assess the situation before replying to any questions.

"I am the one who drives the boat. My brothers and sisters here are the children of the boat's owner," Phú said.

"You! You drive this boat?" The man was shouting, and I was afraid he would hit my brother.

"Yes! I am responsible. Ask anyone in this boat. They can confirm that."

The men still held their guns on my brothers. One man had an ugly smirk on his face, dismissing these city kids with their fair skin and obvious inexperience, as well as the skinny teenage boy who was the boat's driver. I realized that Chú Tư was not in the cabin; Phú wanted to take all the responsibility, acting as though he was fully in charge. This is what Father had instructed him to do to safeguard Chú Tư's identity. Escapees who were caught after their release from political re-education camps often received life imprisonment. For Chú Tư, with his direct connection to the American navy, getting caught would be a disaster.

A man who appeared to be the leader jumped onto the boat at the stern and walked into the cabin. He was holding a pistol but appeared less aggressive and told the others to stop pointing their weapons at my brothers. The man on the deck still aimed his gun through the open door at the passengers trembling in the hold.

"You, you and you. Move!" The leader waved his pistol at me, Hằng Phương and the other woman in the cabin, gesturing toward their ship. The man with the rifle jumped into the hold and told some other women, and a few men, to move to their ship. Those who were picked obeyed quietly. Everyone was terrified into silence.

I moved to the patrol boat and found myself separated from Hằng Phương. I sat down and tried to gag down the tablet that was still stubbornly stuck in my throat. I suddenly thought of the blue Puma bag, which I had left behind in the cabin, the butterfly knife still inside. In my moment of terror, I had forgotten Father's advice to remain calm and use the knife to defend myself.

The deck was spacious, and our guards didn't appear to be very interested in us. Two of them kept an eye on us while the others shouted at the people in the hold of our boat. I covered my ears, trembling as their hostile voices shrieked through the thin wooden hull. I closed my eyes and searched for the silver chain around my neck, a small statue of Phật Bà Quan Âm, the Bodhisattva of Compassion, blessed by the monk at Linh Sơn Temple. Another gift from my father, the figure was made from a crystal skillfully cut to glow with a mixture of purple and teal colours and framed in gold.

I watched the statue sparkle in the sun and prayed for the safety of my siblings and all sixty-six lives whose futures were in the hands of communist policemen in civilian clothes. I could hear others chanting, begging and crying and wondered if our prayers would be heard under this clear blue sky.

Soon after, the policemen allowed us to go back to our boat. The people beside me stood up and began to move quickly. I tried to follow them, but nausea made me dizzy. I tumbled and fell. A policeman came over to me; the sight of his feet made my heart race and the tablet stuck in my throat was finally dislodged. I threw up violently, all over his shoes. I trembled with fear, sure I had provoked his anger and put everyone in greater peril. I closed my eyes, seeing both dark and bright spots dance before me, then felt someone take my right arm and help me climb back onto our boat. I got back to the cabin to find Hằng Phương, all my brothers and everyone else in good shape. The passengers in the hold also appeared to be unharmed.

I learned that they had questioned my brothers and searched our boat for hidden gold or diamonds while they held Hằng Phương and me as hostages. The passengers in the hold had been dispersed to make room for the search.

The policemen went back to their boat and announced that we would either be taken ashore or to Côn Sơn Island, where we would all be placed in prison. They began to tow us at a slow and steady speed as people cried and cursed. A few quietly lowered their heads and prayed.

A woman yelled from the hold, "We must beg them to let us go. Children of the boat owner, you must kowtow to them and beg them to let us go." She emerged on deck, pulling a woman with a bloody wrist—she had been hurt when her jade and gold bracelet was pull off by one of the policemen. They both repeatedly kowtowed, crying and begging the policemen to have mercy.

Other passengers shouted. "Why did she wear such an obviously expensive piece of jewelry while escaping?"

"Stupid! There is no use kowtowing to them. Just pray that we do not get beaten and die in prison!"

I closed my eyes and lay down with my face to the wall, trying to block out the desperate cursing and the horrible swearing. I thought of the fake names that Father gave me and my siblings and tried to rehearse what I had to say when we got to the prison.

My brothers appeared composed. Phú remained at the wheel. Phiên passed around an old fabric bag for the escapees to put inside whatever valuables they had left. I reached inside my bag and put in the thick roll of Vietnamese currency Father had given me; my brothers, sister and Phiên's fiancé did the same. I added my old watch and the Bodhisattva of Compassion with the gold frame. Phán stood by Phiên, who held up the bag to show the policemen. They stopped their ship only long enough to collect it. The two women at the bow continued to cry and beg; people in the cabin and the hold started to pray. The sounds of the chanting of Buddhist scriptures and the prayers to Jesus Christ and the Virgin Mary got louder, filling the air, echoing across the ocean.

Then, a miracle occurred. Our prayers were answered.

The policemen untied the line. Surprisingly, they left us with a pot full of fried rice and gave Phú directions to avoid Côn Sơn Island. To everyone's relief, their ship moved farther away from us, leaving us hopeful again, closer to freedom. The escapees started to cheer, erupting with tears and laughter. Phán passed the first aid kit to the woman with the injured wrist. It took Phú two tries to restart engine. All my brothers asked me if I was all right as I wiped away the tears that kept pouring from my eyes. I laughed a bit hysterically when I thought about the moment I vomited on some policeman's shoes.

Phán handed me my old wristwatch and the pendant of the

Bodhisattva of Compassion. I wonder to this day why the policemen did not take them. The watch was old but there was gold in the pendant. Why did they return it? I never found the answer, but I was thankful for a long time after.

I finally fell into a deep sleep. When I woke up, it was dark. People were asleep in the cabin and the hold. Phú was still holding the wheel and I had a quiet moment to observe him. Years away from Đà Lạt had erased his fair skin tone. Now he was tanned. Only one year older than me, he had inherited Father's wisdom; his expression reflected the enormous responsibilities suddenly thrown upon his young shoulders.

It had been nearly three years since I had seen him. For much of that time he had been by himself, unable to communicate with his family without raising suspicion. Lan Phương had told me that the new guitar that Father bought for him had been his companion. I wanted to tell him that many of his classmates thought he already lived in a Western country. I wanted to say that the sister of one of his classmates told me her brother was relieved that he finally had no competition for the top prizes. I wanted to tell him that I could identify Polaris now, but I did not want to disturb his concentration—one of his hands was on the wheel while the other held the binoculars he was using to examine some dots on the horizon. I looked at the dark purplish sky holding the Big Dipper and recalled seeing the shooting star from under the willow tree. I'd made a wish back then, for everyone to be safe, for a successful escape and, most important of all, for my family to reunite. For the rest of the trip, whenever I could suppress my seasickness, I looked up at the dark sky and waited for another shooting star.

I reached into my bag for a piece of the lime–sugar confection that helped ease my seasickness. I let the sour and sweet taste slowly melt on my tongue, thinking of Father, Mother and my younger siblings, who were probably still at the hotel in Saigon. It had only been a day, but it felt like a long time had passed.

The boat entered international waters and started to take on sea-water. The boisterous men who had initially given Phú trouble now took turns bailing. People in the hold took turns going to the bow or climbing on deck for fresh air. Hằng Phương helped Phiên mix lime drinks for the passengers. Father had prepared many packages of dried rice that turned soft when soaked in water. Phán distributed the drink and the soft rice to everyone in the hold. I had a few sips of lime drink to ease my thirst, but I did not want to eat the rice. The seasickness stubbornly remained, defeating me to the point of total helplessness.

I slipped in and out of sleep, my shallow rest only lasting for two or three hours. I wondered if Phú ever slept or took a rest. Every time I was awake, I saw him at the wheel or emerging from the engine room, covered in oil. The roar of the engine was a cause for opti-mism. Everyone held onto the hope that an international ship would appear and rescue us.

On the fourth day of our voyage, a boy yelled that he'd spotted a ship on the horizon. Chú Tư and Phú used the binoculars to verify that the vessel appeared to be a foreign merchant ship. Other, smaller ships could pose as fishing boats but there was a high prob-ability that the fishermen would turn out to be deadly pirates.

The merchant ship headed toward us, its hull a distinctive red colour, with the Japanese flag flying above the bridge. A few Japanese men stood on deck, carefully observing us. On our deck, some men were cheering, their eyes beaming with new energy. Other passengers, including me, were too seasick to show any reaction. Chú Tư, who was fluent in English from his many years of working with the Americans, spoke with them. People tried to climb up onto the deck from the hold, causing our boat to list dangerously. Chú Tư and all my brothers had to shout commands to keep us from capsizing.

The Japanese sailors told us to go farther south, toward the west, to reach an oil rig. They gave us fresh water and lots of tea bags and filled the tank with fuel. They may have represented civilization in the middle of the vast ocean, but they still abandoned us. Chú Tư was disappointed that they did not do any more to help. It seemed we did not look desolate enough to be rescued. Before they drove their red ship away, they threw over some cigarettes and chocolate bars onto the deck of our boat.

The sea was calm, the waves made by our boat the only ripples. The sun shone down directly with no winds to ease the heat. I looked down into the ocean and was surprised to see that the water was quite clear. I could see the sunrays dancing below the surface, exposing the transparency of the depths, intensifying the confusion of the boat people. Mysterious secrets could be revealed, but death also lurked beneath the shimmering surface. Only the thin wooden hull separated the two.

It took more than a day to go farther south. Our boat reached the oil rig near midnight. It stood in the middle of the sea, a massive operational piece of metal with fire shooting out of one of its chimneys, another sign of hope. Phú docked the boat near a platform and Phán tied our boat to one of the rails. The sea remained calm in the darkness. Lights were turned on, and two foreigners came down the stairs, warning us to stay where we were.

A Westerner stood near the edge of the dock repeatedly shooting an arrow down into the dark sea, practising bow fishing. A few big fish were lying at his feet. He walked over and offered us one, then seemed to realize that we had nothing to cook fish with. He raised a Polaroid camera he was wearing around his neck and took a picture. Once the image came out, he flicked it vigorously and gave it to us.

Many men came up on deck to observe the oil rig. Others were too seasick to care. Our main concern was whether we would be rescued, if the people who worked on this oil rig would want to help us. We learned from Chú Tư that they said we were very near Malaysia. Our boat was still operational, and we appeared to be capable of reaching our destination without their assistance. They gave us fresh water, many bottles of milk and canned food, and warned us about an increase in piracy from Malaysian fishermen. We left that same evening; the next day was our seventh at sea.

The seasickness persisted and I could not eat anything except the lime-sugar lumps. While asleep, my ears either echoed with the sound of the boat engine or the arguments and prayers from the hold. When I was awake, Phú was always there, soaked in oil, trying to maintain the engine or standing by the wheel. Once I heard him tell Chú Tư that he'd changed course after seeing what appeared to be another boat in the distance. Chú Tư calculated and sketched another path on the map. After all, the Japanese ship and the oil-rig workers had left us to defend ourselves on this lawless sea; we could not trust any other vessel to help us. We just had to keep going toward Singapore, our intended destination.

On the eighth day, we entered Malaysian territory, an area dotted with small, deserted islands. The engine, upon which all our hopes rested, appeared to be coming to its end. Our boat was cruising at a low speed on the calm water, Chú Tư at the wheel and Phú in the engine room again, when a Malaysian boat full of fishermen appeared out of nowhere.

As they slowly approached, the woman in the hold yelled, "All the women and girls, stay out of sight. Don't let them see you!" Her voice carried over the sputtering of the engine. "All the men climb up onto the deck. Show them that you are strong and healthy."

The rowdy men quickly equipped themselves with wooden rods and ropes and stood on the deck, showing off their strength. One of the men who had given Phú trouble earlier now swung a hammer back and forth.

Everyone realized that the Malaysian boat might want to assess our ability to defend ourselves. The fishermen observed us with what looked like caution; we could not tell whether or not they were pirates in disguise. One man held up a pot, a gesture indicating an offer of fresh water.

We still had plenty of fresh water and did not want to risk our lives. "Don't let them come near us!" the same woman shouted. I thought of my butterfly knife and reached into my bag to wrap my hand around it.

Phú emerged from the engine room and signalled to Chú Tư that he should drive the boat away from them. He had managed to replace the cable that was causing the trouble.

"Chú Tư, I think we should try to run away from them first, then anchor somewhere among these islands, so I can take another look at the engine. I could only give it a quick fix," Phú said calmly.

As we sped away, the Malaysian boat came after us. Chú Tư gave the wheel to Phú who navigated between the inlets and managed to find a good hiding place. We anchored at a spot near a deserted island and Phú swam under the boat to check the propellor. A few men bailed water from the hold and others kept an eye out for any Malaysian boats. Everyone was anxious and many continued to chant prayers.

It took a few hours for Phú, Phán and Phiên to fix the engine properly. No one needed to announce that the engine had been repaired; we were all familiar with its normal sound and people cheered when it roared back to life. As we cruised through the Malaysian sea, Chú Tư announced that, if everything ran smoothly, we would reach Singapore the next morning.

We entered Singaporean waters on the ninth day. Many other boats, ships and navy vessels were anchored within sight. Phú headed the boat toward a pier while everyone on board crowed their jubilation. We had reached our goal.

The sky was grey and gloomy, suggesting a storm might come at any minute. The wind started to pick up and the waves were getting rougher. Three young men paddled their leisure boat toward us, asking if we could help them get ashore since they had run out of fuel. Phú agreed to help them, and Phán tied their craft to the stern line. It seemed ironic that we were helping others when we were the ones who needed to be rescued.

The Singaporean harbour patrol boat sped toward us, swiftly cutting the line between the boats. They shouted at us through a megaphone, informing us that the Singaporean refugee camp had closed. We had illegally entered Singaporean territory and we had to leave. We would be shot if we did not obey. If it were not for the leisure boat that we had tried to help, they might have been even more hostile. The crew of the patrol boat tied our boat to theirs by the bowline and began pulling us away from the shore. To everyone's dismay, one of the escapees standing by the bow was thrown overboard by a particularly violent jerk. His brother immediately jumped into the water to save him. The harbour patrol continued towing our boat at maximum speed.

People on the deck, in the cabin and in the hold were screaming, their desperate cries filling the air again. Phú acted quickly. As he threw the first lifebuoy ring, he yelled to Phán, "Cut the line, quickly. They're pulling us too fast!"

"It seems like they want our boat to flip so they can drown us!" Chú Tư shouted.

Phán immediately cut the line as Phiên threw another lifebuoy ring into the sea. The brothers were struggling in the water but each managed to grab a ring and swim toward the boat, which was now moving at a slower speed.

The harbour patrol boat stopped a distance away from us, idling to make sure that we left their territory. One officer yelled through the megaphone, telling us that if we headed south, we would reach Indonesia in a few hours. Indonesia was one of the remaining countries that still accepted boat people.

Women sobbed, men cursed and children were frightened, but everyone was relieved that the two men were safely back on board. Phú followed the direction set by the compass and continue to motor toward Indonesia. He pushed the boat to its top speed, passing through the storm and far away from the land that had denied us entry.

CHAPTER 19

MH2284

It was almost dark when we reached Indonesia and were approached by a marine patrol. They were more friendly and knew exactly what to do, leading us to the wooden pier of a small village. After nine days at sea, Phú finally docked our boat.

The Indonesians spoke to Chú Tư in English and asked us to wait on the boat. Everyone was sceptical about whether they truly wanted to help us. Then a man from the village came to greet us with a friendly smile. He stepped onto our boat and explained that he worked for the United Nations High Commissioner for Refugees. "You should all get onto land. Tomorrow, I will arrange a boat to take you to Galang, the refugee camp."

Being allowed to disembark reassured us that the journey had truly ended. People gathered their belongings. I grabbed my blue Puma bag and followed my brothers and sister. It took a moment to regain my balance on solid ground. We were all weary from the long days at sea but many of us cheered as soon as our feet stepped onto the pier. Some knelt and touched their foreheads to Indonesian land.

The Indonesians directed us to the village's pavilion, then broke us into small groups while they decided where to put us for the night. We sat and waited in confusion, discussing whether or not to trust these people. My brothers said we had no choice. The Indonesian man from the UNHCR was wearing a uniform and appeared to be trustworthy.

The villagers came back from their meeting. They had agreed that all the men would stay and sleep in the pavilion. Women and children would shelter at villagers' homes. A stocky woman approached Thu Hà, Hằng Phương and me, signalling us to follow her. We did so with hesitation, unintentionally showing our distrust. She seemed to understand that we did not fully believe her and said something in Indonesian as she waved her hands in the air, mimicking the movement of a boat. We understood that she had hosted other boat people before us. She patted her chest—a gesture to indicate we could place our trust in her.

The path we walked on was dark, but a dim streetlight illuminated houses among the palm trees. The sound of frogs and crickets intermingled with someone singing a lullaby, while the night breeze added to a sense of tranquility and peace.

The woman led us to the back of her house and pointed to a place like a bathhouse, gesturing that she wanted us to take a bath. The water was cold, but after nine days on the boat this was exactly what we needed and we were grateful. I brushed my teeth with the toothbrush that Father had bought and packed for me.

After we finished our baths, the Indonesian lady led us to a room at the back of her house. Here, there was a flat cement block with three colourful sedge mats. We understood that this was where we could rest for the night. She also gave us a basket with three boiled sweet potatoes, but I still did not want to eat. The kindness of this Indonesian villager convinced us that our risky journey was truly at an end. We would be safe from this moment on.

I fell into a deep sleep, but my brain continued to signal that I was moving side to side, up and down with the boat's motion. My body searched for physical balance and my mind vibrated with the waves. My eardrums still reverberated with the sound of the boat engine, now mixed with the sound of frogs and crickets.

Hằng Phương woke me up early the next morning. Sunlight shone through the door as I realized I had just spent my first night in a far-away and unfamiliar land. The kind woman from last night waved her hands and spoke to us in her own language while a few kids looked at us curiously. She wanted us to follow her. I put my bag over my shoulder and walked with my sister.

"When did you wake up? Why didn't you wake me up earlier?" I asked her, complaining that I did not have time to prepare myself.

"You were sleeping like a log. I tried to wake you up twice so we could look for our brothers," Hằng Phương replied grumpily. "I even tried shaking you, but you did not respond. You slept like you were half-dead."

"Where is Chị Thu Hà?"

"She left half an hour ago, to join Anh Phiên at the pavilion. The Indonesian lady took her and came back for us."

The sturdy Indonesian lady walked quickly and we hurried behind her, surrounded by curious children pointing and giggling. I recognized the road we had walked the night before. Along the way, we were joined by other groups of our fellow escapees. I wondered if we should call ourselves escapees or just the countryless. Hằng Phương and I joined Phiên, Thu Hà, Phán and Phi under a palm tree, the guitar and a few of our belongings beside them. The morning breeze rattled the palm leaves and brought us the ocean's salty scent.

"Where is Anh Phú? I don't see him at all," I asked my brothers.

"He decided to stay with the boat last night," answered Phán.

"The Indonesians said that they will take us to a refugee camp in another boat," added Phiên.

A fellow escapee sitting near us said, "You guys should go to the boat and get more of your stuff, the mosquito nets, pots and pans. You may not be able to find or buy things like that at the refugee camp."

Phán turned to her. "We gathered whatever we could yesterday, but the Indonesians won't allow us on the boat anymore. One of them is there right now asking Phú to leave."

I could see our boat from where I sat. It was finally at rest, its engine turned off. An Indonesian man dressed in a uniform was standing by the wheel as Phú emerged from the cabin and hesitantly stepped onto the wooden dock. As he walked toward us, I wondered if he had finally had a full night's sleep, liberated from worrying about everyone's safety. He joined us under the palm tree and leaned against it, his eyes still on the boat. I noticed he was still wearing the same clothes, the ones stained with brown patches and smelling of oil. The Indonesian man on our boat turned on the engine, untied the rope, slowly backed away from the dock and drove away.

"There, just like that. They took our boat. The boat that Father built, after it safely brought us here." Phú finally broke his silence, his voice weary. For the past three years, the livelihood of our family had depended on that boat. For the last nine days, floating on the vast ocean, it had been our bulwark against the unpredictable sea. Sixty-six lives had been decided by it. In a few short minutes, it was gone, leaving us in this unfamiliar land and at the mercy of these complete strangers.

When the boat was no longer visible, Phú rested his skinny body under the palm tree and took a nap. His breathing was tranquil, but he held the small compass tightly. He later told me he hadn't expected to hand over the boat so soon and didn't have time to gather anything else. The compass was his only souvenir of the nearly three years he lived on the boat and worked alongside Father.

Around noon, a transport boat arrived at the dock. Made of steel and aluminum, it seemed designed for sightseeing, with comfortable benches and oval-shaped windows. I doubted if anyone still wanted to enjoy the sight of the ocean with its endless waves. A few men in military uniforms armed with both long and short guns patrolled the boat, either to guard or protect us, while a man in a neat captain's uniform stood by the wheel, his peaked hat on his head, talking through a microphone in a language we did not understand. The villagers signalled us to get on the boat and the tone of the captain's voice reassured us that he would safely bring us to land again.

I reached into my bag and pulled out the sugar lumps mixed with lime. Some had begun to melt and now stuck to the surface of the bag. I scraped off what was left and put it into my mouth. I sat near the door with my head against the window, hoping seasickness would spare me this time. My hand touched the butterfly knife in the bag, and I wondered if I still needed it. Not far from me, Phú slept on a bench, his right arm across his forehead, exactly the way Father slept. It was a position that suggested complex thinking for an unsolvable problem or an unbearable burden; had he fully let go of his responsibilities?

As the boat slowly navigated the narrow passages between islands, I was reminded of one of my high-school geography lessons. Indonesia was a country that consisted of thousands of islands, some of them were unexplored. The teacher had mentioned an interesting detail—the possibility that there were tribes not yet discovered or recorded. In a short while, sixty-six escapees would become refugees on one of these islands.

The sky was a greyish shade when the boat reached the wharf on an island named Pulau Galang, where the UNHCR had established the Galang Refugee Camp. The soldiers gathered us on the pier, spoke to us in English and instructed us to line up before two long tables. At one table, a Vietnamese man sat beside an Indonesian man in civilian clothes, each with papers in front of them. Indonesian soldiers stood behind the other table, which was stacked with packages, sedge mats and umbrellas.

"Who is the owner of the boat, or the individual who commanded the boat?" the Vietnamese man yelled out loud, translating the English sentences spoken by the Indonesian man.

Everyone turned and looked at Phú, who moved past them to the front of the line, Phiên and Phán a few steps behind him. The Indonesian man looked at Phú's young face and slender figure suspiciously.

"You? You owned the boat and commanded the crew?" The Indonesian man raised his eyebrows at Phú. Phiên and Phán stepped closer, guarding their brother, who in truth had commanded the entire trip. Chú Tư signalled for his family, Phi, Thu Hà, Hằng Phương and me to move up until we were all lined up in a group behind my brothers.

"What is the license plate of your boat?" the Vietnamese man translated.

"MH2284! Minh Hải 2284," answered Phú immediately.

"Do you still have any proof or papers to identify the boat?" The Indonesian man still kept his eyes on Phú.

"No, we had to destroy them at the Mekong River, before the boat entered the Pacific Ocean," answered Phú.

"How many people boarded the boat? How many people arrived here on this dock? Did anyone get sick or die? Was anyone buried at sea or thrown overboard?" The Vietnamese man asked the questions without emotion. It seemed a routine procedure for him.

The questions highlighted the complexity of being the boat owner. Since the boat arrived safely, they did not ask for the captain. Instead, they investigated how the boat owners and their associates had treated their fellow escapees on the perilous voyage. Together with luck, the wisdom Phú either inherited or learned directly from Father and the smart decisions he made as a result had protected us all from danger and even death. As I listened to Phú declare that everyone was well fed, healthy and safe, I wondered if everyone truly appreciated what he had achieved.

The Indonesian civilian signalled that we should move to the other table. The soldiers handed each of us a sedge mat woven with several bright colours, a mosquito net and a package that contained food, drink, personal hygiene kits, paper and pen. One bamboo umbrella was distributed to each family. The Vietnamese interpreter wrote all our names onto a list and informed us that we had to memorize the boat's license plate. From this day on, our names were tied to the identity of the boat, MH2284.

The day was nearing dusk. It took a while to record the names of sixty-six people. The wind was getting stronger and people were becoming increasingly impatient, irritated by the noise of whining and crying children. The military men quickly helped us get on their military truck then drove us inland until we could no longer see the ocean. The trucks climbed several hills before stopping in front of two barracks separated from the surrounding forest by a small patch of barren land. This was where we would begin our life as countryless people, waiting to see which nation would decide to accept us.

"You are to stay in these isolation barracks for two weeks in accordance with the quarantine policy. In the next few days, you will receive more supplies," the Vietnamese interpreter said to us before he left with the soldiers. No one stayed behind to guard us.

Each barrack was a long rectangular building with a bare cement floor and four wooden walls. There was one door in each wall and an aluminum roof equipped with gutters that collected rainwater into huge steel barrels. Not far from the barracks, there was a separate cement station for cooking, open to the elements with only a roof on top. Next to it, there were bath stalls and toilets to be shared. There were only two isolation barracks in the whole area, surrounded by mountains and trees. Before this island was turned into a refugee camp, it had been inhabited only by rats and poisonous snakes.

Families and women settled in one barrack. The other was occupied by single men. There was plenty of room for all of the MH2284 boat people. We placed the sedge mats on the cement floor to sit, eat and sleep. We figured out that the coiled incense sticks included inside our packages were to discourage mosquitoes that were fat, abundant and hungry for human blood. At night, we burned the incense and slept under the mosquito nets.

The sound of the dense tropical rain hitting the roof was deafening; we had to scream to hear each other. We also found mung beans and sugar inside the packets and cooked a dessert called *chè đậu xanh*. My brothers took turns playing the guitar while we sang along. There were no books to read, but we could write letters with the paper and pens provided. Every day for the next two weeks was filled with playing guitar, singing, cooking and eating.

I missed Lan Phương, Father and Mother, Phổ, Phấn and the rest of our family back in Vietnam. I realized I had completely forgotten to look for mermaids throughout the nine days on the Pacific Ocean. The endless nausea, constant vomiting and excessive worry made me forget my promise to Lan Phương.

After the quarantine period, we were again transported in military trucks to Galang I, the main refugee camp on the island. The moment we jumped off, we were besieged by huge crowds of Vietnamese refugees looking for their relatives or acquaintances. It was a regular routine for the refugees on the island; everyone yearned for a reunion and nourished a slim hope that their loved ones would also escape Vietnam and miraculously join them.

The sixty-six refugees of MH2284 were divided into different barracks. We were put into Barrack 20, which became our home address for more than half a year. The barracks of Galang I were similar to those of the quarantine site, except each had a wooden platform raised about half a metre above the cold cement floor. The centre had at least one hundred barracks and more were still under construction. The maximum capacity of each barrack was set at sixty and rarely exceeded that number. Some barracks appeared to be less crowded. Barrack 20 was assigned to four families, each of which occupied a quarter of the space and together filled the entire wooden platform. Two windows opened onto the cooking and washing station. Chú Tư's family lived across from us and we often joined his family for dinner.

At night, we still fought hungry mosquitoes and huge rats that would bite human toes if they got a chance. Once, the administrators of the camp set up a contest with rewards for those who caught the most rats and snakes. Many of them were caught, killed and burned on one of the isolated hills located between Galang I and Galang II.

The primary water source was rainwater collected in huge steel barrels situated near the four entrances to each barrack. The refugees also dug wells to collect water and the area around them was often crowded since many people gathered there to wash clothes. People put up plastic tarps with blue and white stripes outside their assigned quarters to create more living space, then used the densely crisscrossed ropes to hang clothes often soaked by the island's daily rain.

I considered that whoever set up the camp, whoever was in charge of running it, thought it was natural and appropriate for refugees to have no privacy. None of the barracks had a lock and everyone's private news—who had passed or failed settlement interviews—was broadcast over loudspeakers. The story of every new arrival, whether lucky or tragic, became public the moment the refugees reached the pier. Immoral and petty men, through their daily gossip, exacerbated the horrendous ordeals that had befallen unfortunate women before their arrival. Mental health support was non-existent.

Well-paved main streets connected several hills. On the top of one hill, a building with a cross was the Protestant church. Not far from it, on another hill close to Barrack 20, the statue of the Virgin Mary stood in front of the Catholic church. Across the valley, where most of the barracks were, we could easily recognize the Buddhist temple's curvy and pointy roof atop another hill. Not far from the Catholic church, a wooden stage was built with a big white screen, partially torn. This was supposed to be a movie theatre but the only film ever shown was Sylvester Stallone's *First Blood*.

Past the Protestant church, new roads were built leading to Galang II, which accommodated refugees already accepted by a third country who were waiting for permanent settlement. The barracks in Galang II were more modern than the ones in Galang I. The sleeping quarters were raised at least seven feet above the ground, with shared stairs built for every two units. Intersecting with the road between Galang I and II was a path leading to a hill where all the modern houses were built for the teachers, policemen and administrators of the camp. A water tower stood high beside a paved parking lot filled with cars, police jeeps and church vans.

Administrative, educational and social activities were concentrated in Galang I. A specific educational area had been built beside the clinic where English classes, ranging from basic to advanced, were divided into morning and afternoon shifts. An audio centre was always packed with keen learners with headphones stuck over their ears. There was a small room called the library connected to one of the classrooms. Next to the medical clinic stood the building housing the UNHCR office, the site of countless interviews that decided the future of the refugees. Next to this building, a small jail nicknamed the "dog den" was attached to the Indonesian police station. The jail cells were mostly empty and anyone who landed in one ignited massive amounts of gossip.

As soon as we were settled, we wrote to let our family know that we were safe but the postal system was not too reliable. Many refugees sent letters to their relatives in Vietnam by entrusting them to people who were leaving the camp to resettle in their new country. It depended on the kindness of these strangers whether or not they would immediately spend part of their first pay cheque to buy the stamps, then to affix them to the piles of envelopes waiting to be sent. It took a while for those letters to reach Vietnam, and chances were most of them would be confiscated at the postal stations by communist officials. Those seized letters often resulted in further investigation and monitoring of the family members left behind.

I often questioned if my parents were receiving the letters that we were sending to them; they had not been able to reply. Then, two months after we arrived at the camp, we heard our names called out, together with our boat identity, from the public loudspeaker. The announcer said that we had to meet the priest at the Catholic church not far from our barrack. Father had found a relatively secure way of sending a letter to us—he sent his letters to Singapore, to a postal box belonging to the priest who made monthly trips to the camp.

We received three letters at once, each written at a different time, a few days apart. The letters were almost identical, as Father was not sure any of them would reach us. Each of them said that the family was well, that they missed us and that we should concentrate on our studies. In one of the letters, Father wrote that Grandmother had passed away peacefully, fifteen years to the day after Grandfather. I found an isolated spot on the church grounds to sob. Despite the hot and humid weather of the tropical island, I felt chills running down my spine.

My Grandmother had a calming aura that warmed the air around her and her shiny silver hair was usually tied in a bun. When she came to help look after Lan Phuong, I admired her hair every morning as she combed it with a comb made of elephant tusk, a gift from her late husband.

"This comb was hand made in a famous village filled with talented sculptors. It gives me comfort whenever I miss your Grandfather," she said in a melancholy voice, gazing into an empty space. All her blouses had an inner pocket specially sewn to securely contain her precious comb.

Grandmother's hair was about a metre long, extending to her knees. She explained that she hadn't cut it since Grandfather passed away eight years ago. "Jolie, for a girl, hair is the symbol of her inner virtue. You need to keep your ebony hair shiny and beautiful," she said as she gently combed my hair. Every evening, she caressed it while she sang beautiful folk songs to put Lan Phương to sleep.

I could not recall any times I had spent with my grandfather. He died when I was a toddler. I recalled seeing his image on the altar while our family vacationed at Mũi Né in 1973: he was wearing a full brimmed hat of the era in which the French invaded Vietnam. Grandfather worked as a barber and a photographer and was well known by many citizens of Mũi Né. He built a photo darkroom in his home where Grandmother often worked alongside him developing film. Now she said she lived only to fulfil her duties to her children and grandchildren. She told me she knew the exact time that she would join Grandfather.

I was curious. "Why do you say you know when you will meet Grandfather again?"

"I will tell you when you are older. You are still too young to understand."

For the first six months of Lan Phương's life, we shared the elephant tusk comb at every sunrise. Every time that comb straightened my hair, I thought of my grandfather and felt his presence: the love he gave to my grandmother, my mother, my aunt and uncles and the grandchildren he never met. Grandmother's long silvery hair was a symbol of her enduring love for him.

Grandmother taught me the secret of keeping healthy hair. She told me to collect the seedpods from the honey locust trees, which fell to the ground and littered the streets of Đà Lạt. While Lan Phương was napping, I helped Grandmother wash her hair with the brown liquid made by boiling these seedpods, carefully blending it into her hair with the elephant tusk comb.

Our time with Grandmother was short but full of love and joy. She steamed delicious sticky rice with mung bean, called *xôi vò*. She cooked delicate seafood dishes from the dried fish and squid that she brought with her. We had fried rice with this famous fish sauce most mornings before walking to school. The food we had while Grandmother stayed with us tasted more delicious than regular meals—she said that where she lived seafood was easier to find and store. She taught me how to make braided tofu and preserved cabbage. Every dish was prepared with delicacy and love.

One Sunday, Grandmother decided to take a break from looking after Lan Phương to visit a relative who lived in the countryside on the outskirts of the city.

"Jolie, do you know this address?" she asked, showing me the address on a letter.

"Of course, Grandmother. My classmate lives in this area. I have visited her house a few times to help her with homework," I replied with enthusiasm, excited by the idea of a break and a trip with Grandmother. Then I recalled that we would have to go past the city cemetery. "Grandmother, we have to go past Mã Thánh cemetery. That part of the road is scary!"

"We'll bring some incense with us," she replied.

It turned out to be an awfully long and tiring walk for Grandmother, who kept resting along the way, massaging her knees and asking if we were there yet. When we got to the cemetery, I wanted to run past, but Grandmother could not walk any farther. She sat on the pavement right beside the cemetery.

"Grandmother, we cannot rest here. The ghosts are scary. They are going to come after us." I tried to pull her off the ground.

"No, Jolie. Let me rest here for a while," she said calmly. "The spirits are not going to harm us if we respect them."

I was about to cry.

"Jolie, light some incense and put it on top of a few graves near here. The spirits will be pleased with that. Don't be scared."

I clung to her, imagining ugly, grinning, creepy ghosts about to emerge from their tombs. "There, there, Jolie. Don't be frightened. The dead can see us. We cannot see them, but we can feel them." She hugged me tightly and massaged my shoulder. "The dead are not scary. They linger on this earth because they love their relatives. They miss their families and want to be with them."

Grandmother lit the incense and stood up with me. Together, we placed sticks on top of the graves near the road. I felt a chill, sensing spirits were watching me.

That evening, while rocking Lan Phương, instead of singing folk songs, Grandmother decided that I was old enough to hear her secret. She whispered to me. "Jolie, let me tell you a secret. I often see your Grandfather in my dreams. Eight years ago, the moment before he died, he said that he would come to take me with him on the same day that he died, fifteen years later. After I have fulfilled my responsibilities as a parent and a grandparent."

I did not want to believe her, but I took her seriously, counting how many more years that would be. I cried and told Mother and Father. Mother said Grandmother deeply grieved for Grandfather, missed him tremendously, and that this story was her coping mechanism. Father did not comment, but I knew he was analyzing the details.

In the letter, Mother also wrote about what happened the day before Grandmother died. In the weeks before, Grandmother had been ill, but not seriously so. Still, Father remembered what Grandmother said and insisted Mother depart for Mũi Né. Mother, together with her siblings, performed a memorial service for Grandfather on the anniversary of his death. That evening Grandmother died in her sleep, a smile on her face.

CHAPTER 20

INFLECTION POINT

Every two weeks, each family or group of individuals received a portion of rice and salty dried fish, which formed the basis of each meal. Some refugees could afford to rent a piece of land, buy seeds from the Indonesians and plant vegetables they sold at a profit. There were also a few street stalls that sold canned foods, bread, clothes and a variety of other products for daily living. The merchandise was brought in from the mainland by Indonesian proprietors. These goods were luxuries that were unaffordable for us.

We were rarely given fresh produce, so Hằng Phương cut a small strip of gold from the piece Mother had sewn inside the lining of her undershirt to buy vegetables. I used my butterfly knife to help her cut them up. But we also needed to buy two sets of clothes, sandals and basic personal hygiene items that were not provided in the supplies. The gold did not last for the fourteen months we remained in the camp.

After a few months, I developed severe edema from a lack of nutrition, with a high fever. Both my feet became so swollen they looked like they belonged to an elephant. A Vietnamese doctor sent me to the medical clinic for further treatment. I didn't want to go but had no choice—poor health would negatively affect the resettlement process for all of us. The clinic mostly treated minor ailments, and patients with major illnesses would be transported by boat to a hospital in a bigger city, then transferred back to the clinic for recovery. It was managed by two Indonesian nurses under the direction of a foreign Caucasian doctor, with a female Vietnamese doctor volunteering as an interpreter. When I was admitted, the Indonesian nurse gave me six black pills to swallow and settled me in a room with four beds. My sister and brothers were not allowed to stay with me, but Hằng Phương, who had been studying to be a nurse, knew the Vietnamese doctor. She told her that she could visit me the next day. I longed for the soothing presence of Father and Mother who used to put their hands on my forehead to feel my temperature. Father always stayed up all night if any of us were sick.

The nurse brought me some food, picking it up with her fingers to feed me. I hesitated at first, then remembered that Indonesians don't use chopsticks. But before I could open my mouth, the patient in the next bed began to vomit violently and profusely, her body curled by the force of her heaving.

She screamed and cried, blood coming from her mouth, disturbing the women in the other two beds. They sat up and began to shout, their skeletal figures swaying back and forth, shaking bald heads with hollowed eyes. Their loud cries disturbed the patient in the room next door, who punched the wall and began wailing. The other nurse ran into the room, followed by the Vietnamese doctor. They managed to calm the vomiting woman, but the eerie wailing and the thumping sounds continued.

I overheard the staff talking outside the room and learned that the patient in the next bed always vomited at the sight or smell of food. Her boat had drifted for months on the sea and the other escapees had all died from hunger and thirst. She and the other two patients survived by eating the corpses of their fellow escapees. The patient next door had apparently just had an abortion. Her boat had encountered a Malaysian fishing vessel and, instead of being rescued, the

Malaysian fishermen robbed the men, killed the babies and elders, then raped the women, things they learned from Thai fishermen, who had been the first predators. Her children and her husband were killed; she survived only to become pregnant.

Now I understood why Father had bought me the butterfly knife and insisted I practise using it. I understood why he told me to aim that knife firmly, to try to slash the part between the evil man's legs.

The night before we left, Mother had pulled me aside to hand me a thick, red-stained pad. "Jolie," she had said, "wear this, even though you don't have your period. This liquid is medical grade disinfectant. It is safe to wear it for the entire trip."

Now I understood why Phú turned off the lights and let the boat feel its way through the darkness of the open sea, changing course if he saw a light in the distance. Why he turned the wheel and gunned the engine if, looking through the binoculars, he saw any ships during the day. I thought about the Malaysian boat that had approached us, tempting us with a huge jar of fresh water before chasing us. Even though I had just turned seventeen, I had been very sheltered and had no real understanding of evil. That all changed in one night.

The despair and anger of these women entered my body; my fever got worse and my head began to hurt. The Indonesian nurse gave me more black pills to swallow. I felt myself slipping away, my consciousness existing in a strange medium filled with a mixture of darkness and illumination. I felt I was in the presence of Death.

I am Death.
I save souls.
Invisible to humans
Who only see me
At the moment of their death.
Many Vietnamese have fled
Their homeland.
Many have died.
Buried deep in the watery abyss.
Vanished, in silence.
Forever unheard by other humans.
Only I witnessed their misery.
Only I heard their cries.
Only I completed their journey.
Unseen . . . to be seen.
Unheard . . . to be heard.

I came to save their souls as the howling wet winds tore their tarps under a dark, purplish sky, the gigantic and unforgiving waves burying their disabled boat in a massive watery grave a few days after they left their homeland's shore. I pulled them from the darkness of the deep salty water and saved these drowning souls. They thanked me, but the moment they realized their bodies were trapped at the bottom of the ocean, they begged me to release them and to let them live. Why, they asked, had they to die such a sudden death? In some boats, no one survived to tell the world of their last horrible moments—Mother Nature had silenced them. No one lived to tell their relatives how and where they died, and their loved ones waited, waited, longing to hear news that never came.

There were times when I grew weary of the slower demise of other groups of desperate escapees. These were the ones who were dying from thirst and hunger. I was present, beside them, but invisible as the cruel heat of the sun assaulted their curled bodies, intensifying the stench of urine and excrement. They could only sit in silence, shoulder to shoulder, without enough space to stretch their legs. None of them had the strength to wail; no more liquid formed in their tear ducts. They kept their dignity as they died, their souls happily leaving their ravaged bodies. These souls gladly clung on to me, relieved to be released from their prolonged suffering.

When collecting the souls of those destroyed by living devils—Thai or Malaysian fishermen whose catch of the day was satisfying their greed and sexual desire—I sometimes felt conflicted.

These destroyers hunted in the unforgiving sea, robbing, killing, raping, kidnapping and then sinking the wrecked boats to drown the evidence. They killed the elderly, men, children and babies. They raped the women and girls, then sold them to brothels or killed them. Their acts destroyed these souls and they wrestled to be released from me. These souls thought they could still save their parents, their wives and their babies, or could survive to take revenge for the injustice they suffered. I wanted to let them go, just for a moment, so they could have their vengeance, but I could not. I was bound by duty. I chained those vengeful souls together and hauled them away even as those monstrous Thai and Malaysian men celebrated their victories.

It was no struggle to collect the souls of those murdered by fellow escapees, their judgment impaired by lack of water and food. Hunger and thirst brought out the ugliest traits in these humans, their minds

141

consumed by a war of morals. The souls of their victims were speech-less, eerily silent when I saved them. These souls died again, when they watched their lifeless bodies cut up and boiled in seawater to feed others, their blood used to slake the thirst of others. Gently, I carried these souls away.

On the Pacific Ocean, my mission was to save all these souls: the bewildered, drowning souls, the starving and tormented souls, the vengeful and helpless souls, the violated and horrified souls. On this island, and in this refugee camp, hopeless souls continue to seek me out, begging me to release them from their miseries.

Jolie, I am Death! I am present in this room, and I am waiting . . .

"Is my sister's fever getting better?" I heard Hằng Phương ask the Vietnamese doctor.

"She is sweating a lot. I think she can leave the clinic today. It is better for her to rest in the barrack," the doctor replied, checking my temperature.

I found myself more aware of what was going on around me and opened my eyes to find myself in a different room, one with only two beds, the other empty. It was nearly dark outside; I had slept for more than a day. I was soaking in my own sweat and guessed the black pills had worked. I realized that I could lift my feet, which showed signs of returning to their original shape.

The nurse came back with a bowl of seaweed soup on a tray. She reminded me of the kind lady who had given us sweet potatoes the night we landed. The nurse handed me the bowl of soup and, relieved not to be fed by hand, I drank it. I begged the doctor to let me leave quickly as my memory of the wailing and the heart-wrenching scene of the day before returned with full force.

"The pills I gave her worked well. I'll sign the discharge form and prescribe more pills for her," the Vietnamese doctor told the Indonesian nurse.

Before I was discharged, the nurse took me to the bathroom to shower. I realized I had not been in a real bathroom since leaving the hotel in Saigon. The walls were covered in white tile and the water flowed by a turn of the faucet. There was also a mirror, which had become another luxury item. I had not looked at myself in the mirror for a long time. We did not have any mirrors in the barrack; perhaps that was for the best. The mirror installed here reflected the face of Death. I couldn't forget those skeletal patients with their hollow and miserable eyes. Death had taken their souls but left their gaunt bodies as evidence.

On the road from Galang I to Galang II, between the two camps and not far from the Protestant church, there was a place the refugees called Galang III, the haunted and deserted land where the dead were buried. It was not decent enough to be referred to as a cemetery—some of the graves were marked with names on crosses made of sticks, the characters scribbled in charcoal, not even lined up straight. Other graves were just a hump of dirt above the flat surface. All kinds of tropical weeds and tall grasses grew around them. Some of the boat people had escaped without family and died alone in the camp, with no one to give them a proper burial or to care for their graves. A few had killed themselves out of despair after not being accepted to settle in a new country. I heard a rumour that the women I encountered at the clinic had died. One had reportedly committed suicide. I could not help but believe she had successfully sought Death, whose presence seemed to linger within the white walls of the clinic, but I hoped that what I heard was not true.

Every time I walked past Galang III, besides feeling scared, I thought about how lonely and sad those souls felt. In fleeing Vietnam, all escapees chose the hope of life while embracing the possibility of death. They sought life in the darkness and saw death in the light. This camp was the place where the inflection point of life would be defined—for each of us it would either curve up or dip down. After risking their lives across the ocean, the lives of these refugees had plunged down. Their life had ended before their freedom began.

Delegations from the United States, Canada and Australia regularly visited the camp to review applications, interviewing refugees to decide whether or not they qualified for resettlement in their countries. Every time I walked pass the UNHCR building, I reflected on how a few nods or a few words could so significantly change a refugee's life. I had seen families and people walk out of the building with joy, a contrast to those who came out wearing disappointed expressions.

Chú Tư's family was immediately accepted by the American Delegation since he had worked for the US navy. They left for the United States after only four months at the camp and settled in Chicago. Our applications were rejected outright by all three delegations during the first few months. We were not even granted an interview. We did not fit into the category of being able to enter the workforce immediately to support ourselves soon after we resettled. We also did not have any relatives who had already settled in any of these countries to strengthen our status. The typical stay for most refugees was around six months; our stay lasted for fourteen.

Father searched ceaselessly for a way he could to help us to get a connection in America, Canada or Australia. In his letters, he gave us names of people to write to. He mentioned the names of distant relatives and acquaintances to whom he had sent money in exchange for their help. I don't know how he found these contacts, and we were never sure what happened to their offers of assistance. But his relentless efforts finally saved us. We were called over the loudspeaker to meet a pastor at the Protestant church. Father had contacted him through an acquaintance and sent a letter asking for his help. The pastor informed us that he had sent our names to a man named John Smith, an alderman for a city called Hamilton, who was the founder of a charity called The Mountain Fund to Help the Boat People. Not long after that, we received a postcard from Mr. Smith telling us that this charity had decided to sponsor us privately. We would resettle in Hamilton, Ontario, Canada. His kind words marked the beginning of new hope.

Our names were again called out from the camp loudspeaker one morning, this time to inform us that we should show up at the UNHCR building the following day for an interview with the Canadian delegation. At first, I did not believe this news, until my brothers and sister screamed with joy. Phi asked me to come with him to look for books about Canada at the library he frequently visited. Months of hopeless waiting had ended and we did not want to take any chances. We found two books left on the shelf to check out. That evening, we all gathered eagerly to rehearse what we could be asked and to prepare our answers. We put on our best appearances and, for the first time in a long time, wished that we could have a mirror. I felt a strange anxiety, a factor filtered out from fear.

Surprisingly, our interview was short and straightforward. A man and two women sat across the table from us. They were pleasant and asked simple questions about our names and how long we had been staying at the camp. It turned out that, because we had been accepted for private sponsorship, this was just a formality. The lady smiled as she reached for a stamp and pressed it seven times, the red ink adding the word "Accepted" to each of our files. The exact and only word that was needed to secure our future.

After staying for six months at Galang I, we were finally allowed to transfer to Galang II, where our living arrangements and status were upgraded. We had a relatively private living space and knew for certain what country we would migrate to. Mr. Smith sent us a few more letters. He wrote encouraging words on beautiful cards printed with the flowers of Canada, and enclosed some Canadian currency.

CHAPTER 21

EULER'S IDENTITY

Leonhard Euler derived the most remarkable formula in mathematics: $e^{i\pi} + 1 = 0$, Euler's Identity. A transcendental number e (2.71828...) raised to a power of i (complex or imaginary number $\sqrt{-1}$) times pi (3.14159...), plus 1, equals *zero*. Some call it the most beautiful equation in mathematics because it can be applied to many aspects of real life. How could a number raised to a power end up equal to negative one, and the subsequent result equal zero? The various mathematical theorems used to prove this argument are lengthy. However, at the camp, it was simple to make a connection—a risky effort boosted by the power of courage and hope, but adding the factor of fate, could result in failure and lead to nothing.

In each of the letters that we received from our parents, Father never missed an opportunity to remind us of the value of education. They were a source of encouragement and reminded us to concentrate on mastering the English language and spending time at the educational compound was our main activity. We studied all the English courses offered at the camp until only the English teacher training courses were left. It seemed like the curriculum developers did not think anyone would stay at the camp long enough to finish all the levels. We passed the entrance exam to enroll in those courses, unexpectedly learning to become instructors. Books were rare and we ran out of advanced English books to read. I decided to improve

147

my English by reading a Bible I got from the church; it was printed in both English and Vietnamese.

I missed the sound of chalk moving on the blackboard, along with the voices of my teachers. I never realized that sound was so beautiful and so precious, and I regretted the times that I let my thoughts wander out of the classroom's windows during math lessons. My mind had been preoccupied with the secret plan for fleeing the country and I had rebelliously questioned if those math formulas would be relevant to my life. I had begun to visualize my family's situation as a sinusoidal graph on a Cartesian plane—how our lives were impacted by uncertainty, by my parents' battle to maintain the daily struggle as a smooth and continuous curve. The sine curve moved up and down from the positive quadrant to the negative quadrant, reached its maximum point, then attained its minimum point, repeating the pattern to the infinity. My parents had been wealthy and successful then, with a change of regime, were thrown into poverty and labelled as bad elements.

During the eight-month wait for our resettlement to be processed, we walked to the education complex at Galang I every morning. Phiên, Phán and Phú were all assigned English classes to teach. Phi enrolled in the advanced science class taught in English. Hằng Phương volunteered at the clinic. I volunteered at the audio centre. Whenever I had free time, I listened to the tapes until there were no more tapes to listen to. We got paid a few hundred rupees, Indonesian currency, every two weeks for our volunteer work and used this little bit of money to buy bread to add to our meals.

Every Sunday, we were allowed to go to the beach. It took about an hour to walk through the forest to reach a long stretch of a beautiful sand. On most Sunday afternoons, except during the heavy rains, the camp emptied as everyone went to the beach to collect seaweed or catch little crabs to supplement their meals. I looked forward to spending time there every weekend. We brought the guitar and water and bread for a picnic and vented our homesickness by singing songs musicians had composed in praise of our newfound freedom, songs that were played over the loudspeaker every evening. I would walk along the shore, missing Lan Phương and the rest of my family in Vietnam, remembering our last days together at the hotel in Saigon.

Mother had had to come home to convince Lan Phương to leave Đà Lạt without me. At almost seven years old, she was old enough to understand what Father planned and eventually agreed. More than a month later, we had been so happy to reunite. She had gotten taller and seemed more mature. Her skin was tanned from living on the boat with Mother, Father and Phú. She had described the boat to me in detail as I was the only one of my siblings who had never seen it.

I thought a lot about that last day in Saigon. I remembered Mother telling me that she had talked to Lan Phương so that she would not cry when I left without her. I remembered her talking in an uncharacteristically soft tone while she caressed my hair. "Wear your blue hat with the brim. You have such fair skin. Your cheeks always glow in the sun." I remembered her turning away, walking quickly to her room to hide her emotion. I knew she did not want both of us to cry.

I remembered following Father out of the hotel, wearing my blue brimmed hat as instructed, my blue Puma bag slung across my shoulder. I remembered walking down the stairs to the courtyard and looked up to see Lan Phương, Phố and Phấn standing on the balcony watching us leave, a silent goodbye.

Most of all, I remembered cuddling in the bed with Lan Phương as we whispered promises to each other. "Chị Jolie, remember to look for mermaids. Anh Phú drives the boat so well. Ask him to stop the boat when you see a mermaid."

"Yes, Lan Phương. I promise to look for a mermaid." I couldn't find any other words. Tears were pouring from the corners of my eyes, hidden by the dark.

"Don't be scared, Chị Jolie. Anh Phú will protect you. Make sure you write to me. Mother says we will be together again."

I did not keep that promise; I had forgotten all about mermaids on the boat. Walking along the seashore, I imagined finding a mermaid who lived behind the coral under the rumbling waves but who had emerged to observe the humans on the beach with curiosity. I dug under the white sand to look for the big seashells, but I found few. They must all have been collected by the children of the camp. Perhaps on this beach, in this land of freedom, the creatures who lived in those shells had no sad spirits to leave behind.

I would watch the tide push the waves onto the sand, only to draw back moments later. Some of the fragile white foam was absorbed into the sand, some went back into the sea. In the end, everything boiled down to the meeting and parting, living and dying. Across this ocean, on a far horizon, priceless freedom awaited those who could pull themselves through by faith, resilience and perseverance. For others, Euler's Identity decreed that their willpower and fearless efforts would result in a zero.

The Sunday before we left the camp, we took our last trip to the beach. This time I took the butterfly knife with me. Sitting on a rock and letting the waves wet my feet, I flicked the blade open, recalling the lesson in self-defence that Father taught me. My heart saddened as I remembered the agonized wails of the patient intermittently punching the wall at the clinic. I never met her, but her misery echoed the worst of mankind and vibrated with the excessive cost of freedom. I secured the spring latch to forever hold the sharp blade closed. I walked further down the beach, gathered all my strength and threw the butterfly knife into the ocean.

Father's vision opened the path for us to live freely in the larger world. His courage gave us wings so that we could fly into our brighter future.

CHAPTER 22

THE LAND OF THE WEST

We arrived in Hamilton, Ontario, Canada, in July of 1984.

Stepping out of the security door at Toronto Pearson International Airport, we were greeted by John Smith and a few charity members from the Mountain Fund to Help the Boat People. Mr. Smith asked us how our flight had been and then looked at a paper that listed our names. His empathetic eyes looked at each one of us: seven skinny individuals with only a tiny carry-on bag each slung over our shoulders.

"Let me know who you are, after I pronounce each of your name. Let's start with the youngest: Phi."

Mr. Smith then tried to pronounce the rest of our names but stopped when one of the charity members, who was Vietnamese, laughed. "You practised for hours while driving here, John, but you still cannot get them right," he said.

"I think I should just call you all by Fee, Fi, Fo, Fum, since your names all start with a Ph...." Everyone laughed while we tried to catch on. Sensing that we were overwhelmed and did not fully get the joke, Mr. Smith continued, "Later on, perhaps in a short time, you shall tell me what fairy tale the phrase Fee-Fi-Fo-Fum is from and who said it."

We settled into a three-bedroom townhouse arranged by the charity. Thu Hà, Hằng Phương and I shared one room, Phiên and

Phán had another, while Phú and Phi took the third. The rent and the living expenses were covered by the charity for one month. After that, we would be on our own. During that first month, charity members visited us weekly to bring used clothing, essential furniture and food. We were given bus passes and directions about using the bus, which became our main means of transportation.

I was surprised by the high humidity of the summer months. In the book I read at the camp, Canada was mainly portrayed with images of wintery snow and autumns with red or yellow maple trees. Looking at the beautiful photos, I wondered how people survived in such cold temperature and imagined a new life of working and living in a gigantic freezer.

After two weeks, we all found jobs working on a farm, except for Phi, who we considered too young for labour. Early each morning, a man picked us up in his van and drove for about one hour to a farm near Niagara Falls, then drove us back in the afternoon. I still had my blue brimmed hat and welcomed its protection from the sun. While working in the fields, I kept thinking about the piece of farmland that my parents purchased at Trại Mát, where Father taught us to grow and harvest a variety of crops. I remembered him picking up a handful of dirt, rubbing it between his fingers and telling us to value what nature had provided for humans. That piece of farmland had also been confiscated by the communist government.

Our drive to the farm took us past fields of grapevines, sparking another memory. When I was old enough to notice, I found quite a few empty glass jars beside the rice chest. Some of them were used to store fish sauce, but their main function was to contain red wine. Once Father allowed all of us to taste it, just a tiny sip for the younger ones. He said when he and Mother retired from operating the pharmacy, he wanted to establish a vineyard and produce wine. On those humid days working on the farm, my mind rewound back to the time Father shared his ambition with us. While taking a moment to rest, I would look at the long stretches of farmland, imagining one day Father's dream would come true in this land of the west.

Our farming jobs only lasted for the summer months. In the fall, Phiên, Thu Hà and Hằng Phương got full-time jobs working at a sewing factory, and Phán found work at a bakery. Between them, they covered all our living expenses. They enrolled in English courses offered in the evening, while Phú, Phi and I registered to attend a high school that was a twenty-minute walk from the townhouse. Phú and I began in Grade 11, while Phi started in Grade 9. We were the first Vietnamese immigrants enrolled at this high school.

Our first appointment with the guidance counsellor, Mr. Reed, was mainly a friendly conversation to test our communication skills. It was clear to him that we all wanted to go to university, so he gave us kind advice that shaped our path in education. He organized our schedules so that Phú and I could complete all the Advanced English courses from Grade 9 to Grade 12 during the two years we would be at the school.

In my English class, we began studying Shakespeare's *The Merchant of Venice*. My essays and assignments received no grades, only red ink crossing out words and underlining sentences. I decided to talk to my teacher.

"May I ask why I did not get any actual grades for my submitted work?"

"I don't think I can grade your work. It is full of grammar errors."

"I will try to improve the grammar."

"This advanced class is not for you to improve grammar."

"Should I be enrolled in the Applied English class?"

"No. I don't think your English is good enough for that class either. You should go back to take Grade 5 English."

"Grade 5?"

"Yes, I really mean Grade 5."

On the way to the high school, there was an elementary school that I had hardly given any thought to. But now I started to notice it. I often enjoyed my walks to and from school but the walk home seemed particularly long that day. I stopped at the elementary school and observed it for a long time.I thought of Lan Phương, missing her and thinking that if she were here with me, she would be enrolled in this public school. I remembered sitting with her in her Grade 1 class, learning everything I already knew. I doubted that this school would help improve my grammar.

For a few nights, I slept with my right arm over my forehead. Then I decided to approach my English teacher again. He asked me, "Have you thought about switching to the Grade 5 English class?"

"Yes, I have. But I will not do that."

"Why not?"

"Please give me grades for my submitted work. If I fail, then I will retake the course."

I studied even harder to improve my grammar. At the end of the semester, I received my report card with a grade of 79 percent and the comment, "Her grammar will never be perfect."

After school, we all found part-time jobs. I worked every Saturday as a clerk in a yarn store owned by Mr. and Mrs. MacLeod. Inside the store was a post office, mainly run by Mr. MacLeod. I often mailed letters back home from this post office, buying stamps with the money I earned.

Phú used some of the money he earned from farming to set up a woodworking shop in the basement of the townhouse, where he made exquisite wood-burned picture frames, pencil holders and name plaques. The skill Father had taught us during school holidays now became a small business. Next to the woodshop, Phi set up his painting corner and spent most of his free time producing oil paintings. Mrs. MacLeod displayed the wooden products and oil paintings in a bay window at the front her store and sold them with no commission. We received all of the proceeds.

In addition to attending school and working Saturdays at the store, I got myself a work-from-home job: crocheting. A lady came by the house once a month and dropped off a bag full of yarns, with patterns to crochet wool hats. The skill I had learned from Mother became useful as a source of income. Mrs. MacLeod taught me how to read English crocheting instructions and to follow the required patterns. Once in a while, I saw the hats I had crocheted displayed in department stores.

Shortly after Phán started his full-time job at the bakery, he started the sponsorship application for Father, Mother, Phố, Phấn and Lan Phương to immigrate to Canada. With additional income records from Phiên and Hằng Phương, the application was approved. I sent the sponsorship papers by registered mail from Mr. McLeod's post office.

Communication improved after we settled in Canada. We received mail more regularly and realized that most of our letters sent from the refugee camp had either been confiscated or lost. We all had to be careful about what we wrote since the government could use our words against our parents. Father and Mother rarely mentioned the difficulties the rest of the family had to endure—frequent unannounced visits from badgering communist policemen, and worse.

We wanted to send the money we had saved to Vietnam to help. There were no legal channels to do this, so we came up with our own solution— hiding American dollars inside pencils. Phú used his tools to cut the eraser at the end of a pencil, then drilled out the lead to create a hollow compartment. He rolled a bill to fit it inside the hole, then glued the eraser back into its original place. We mixed the pencils in with school supplies and other cheap stuff to avoid raising the suspicion of officials who would open the package once it reached Vietnam. To alert the family, we wrote a letter with a hidden message:

> Dearest Father, Mother, Phổ, Phấn and Lan Phương,
>
> . . . these pencils are the gifts for Phổ, Phấn and
> Lan Phương to practise their handwriting. The lead
> inside these pencils is dark enough and soft, no need
> to press hard while writing. Therefore, they will help
> tremendously. At the same time, they will gently help
> the hand to perfect the calligraphy. Do not give these
> pencils to anyone or share them with our relatives . . .

We included enough contradictory details to make Father and Mother notice. We knew that Phổ and Phấn had passed the age of practising calligraphy, while Lan Phương still had to. And it was out of the ordinary for us to suggest Father not share presents with our relatives.

Years later, Mother told us that Father immediately noticed that something was odd about our letter. He broke a pencil in half and found the tightly rolled one-hundred-dollar bill.

In his reply to our first package, Father reassured us:

> Dearest Children,
>
> . . . We received all the presents that you sent. Phổ,
> Phấn and Lan Phương are very happy. The pencils
> indeed helped tremendously with practising calligraphy.
> I could not help but worry that you are working hard to
> send the presents to your brothers and sisters, and, at the
> same time, have to keep up with your studies . . .

After the first try, we wrote other letters with hidden codes such as: "Let us know when Phổ, Phấn and Lan Phương run out of pencils," or "Should we send three pencils per month, on a regular basis?"

Every Saturday, I enjoyed my forty-five-minute walk to the yarn store. On my lunch break, I would cross the street to the grocery store and buy a few items for dinner. On one of my first visits, a store clerk approached me.

"Hey, you! You should buy bananas and lots of them."

Even though bananas were not on the list that Hằng Phương had given me, I picked some up. My lunch would have an additional item: a banana. After dinner, my brothers and sister enjoyed the rest.

Each Saturday, the same store clerk would tell me to buy bananas. I wondered why he said this with a smirk on his face. One time, he even put them inside my shopping cart. I ended up with quite a few bananas. I had about twenty minutes left on my lunch break so when I returned to the store, I took a banana out of the grocery bag and also offered one to Mr. and Mrs. MacLeod.

"Jolie, I notice you buy lots of bananas. Is that your favourite fruit?" asked Mrs. MacLeod.

"No, mango is. But each time I go to the grocery store, a clerk keeps telling me to buy bananas. He even put them inside my shopping cart."

Mrs. MacLeod raised her voice a bit. "Really, hmm…, hmm…, every time, huh…?"

The following week, Mrs. MacLeod asked her husband to look after the store and told me that she wanted to go to the grocery store with me. She then asked me to indicate discreetly the store clerk who kept telling me to buy bananas. I pointed him out to her, then walked down the aisles buying all the items on my list. Mrs. MacLeod didn't buy anything, but she had a conversation with the store clerk. After that day, he never bothered me again.

The members of the charity often dropped by to visit and brought us second-hand coats for the upcoming winter. Mr. Smith remembered our names and we learned that the "Fee-Fi-Fo-Fum" phrase came from an old English fairy tale, *Jack and the Beanstalk*. Our drama high school teacher, Mr. Cooke, also visited us, bringing boxes of canned food. He was in charge of extracurricular activities for the students who volunteered for food drives. Each time he came by, he stayed awhile and explained different aspects of Canada culture.

In the middle of October, the maple leaves turned yellow to announce autumn had arrived. Mr. Cooke visited again and asked if we had any ideas about Halloween. He explained that Halloween was the day for souls to come back to visit their homes or for the souls to leave for the otherworld. People set fires to scare away the evil spirits and wore masks and costumes to disguise themselves among witches, goblins and demons. He warned us to have candies ready to treat all the goblins, witches and demons who might visit our house, or they would trick us. I thought Halloween was the festival for the dead, the complete opposite of the practice in Vietnam.

A week later, Mr. Cooke came back with a box of costumes and a pumpkin. On Halloween night, our little townhouse was full of laughter and excitement. We lit a candle inside the hollow pumpkin carved with a suitably scary face. Phú and Phi dressed up as medieval knights and I disguised myself as a bear. We put on a playful act to scare Phiên, Thu Hà, Hằng Phương and Phán before leaving on our mission to trick or treat. They stayed home, enthusiastically giving candies to those who showed up at the doorstep. I remembered the chicken thief and the catastrophe that had befallen him and his family. I hoped that he had escaped Vietnam to freedom and, instead of stealing a chicken, was also having fun collecting treats.

The day I saw snow for the first time, I also received my first letter from Lan Phương. Reading it through eyes blurred with tears, I realized that all the letters I had written to her from the refugee camp had been either lost or confiscated. She wrote as if she had never heard from me.

Dear Chị Jolie,

Today, I am writing to you, so my letter can be put together with the letter that our parents want to send to all my brothers and sisters. I am trying to write as neatly as possible, so my handwriting will be nice compared to the beautiful writing of my older brothers and sisters. Thank you for the doll you sent. I love the doll and play with it every day. But I play with it by myself, not having you to play with me. I miss you and miss the time we played together, telling each other our made-up stories. I miss your guitar playing. I still sing without music from the guitar.

Do you remember you drove me on your bicycle to buy bread from the stall near the movie theatre? Since you left, the bread stall is no longer there.

Do you remember we hid the bread in your school bag, so we could eat it together in bed while reading our bedtime stories?

Do you remember the story, *The Little Mermaid*? I cannot find the book that we had anymore. It is no longer hidden in the rice chest. I think we have lost the book.

Do you remember I cried a lot and would not let you go to school? You put me on your back and carried me to your school. I remember I sat in your Geography class. The teacher described the continents across the Pacific Ocean. Now the two of us are separated and live in two different parts of the world.

I heard from Mother and Father that Anh Phú

drove the boat on the ocean for nine days. While you were on our family boat, did you see any mermaids? Did you try to look for them? I heard that you have to try to look for them so that they will let you see them.

Will you write the letter to me, just for me, and tell me all that? Tell me about your adventure on the sea on our family's boat. I want to find the mermaids too. They live in the ocean, and they will swim along with the boat. You will see them if you look hard enough.

Did you find any more cowrie shells? I think about the one that Father gave us, we need another one to make a pair. So, the two of them can be together, like us, we were always together. Remember, Chị Jolie, we promised to be "together" forever!

I will study hard, study English, so someday I will go to Canada to be with you!

Love you, Chị Jolie.

Your sister,

Út – Lan Phương.

I wrote back but, once again, she never received my letter.

CHAPTER 23

ANCHORLESS

How can I begin?

It is hard to answer questions of "why" and "what if." The last-minute decision to not escape as a family in 1983 became a fatal choice two years later.

When we returned to Đà Lạt, word quickly spread through the neighbourhood and the schools that my children had escaped. A month later, we received word that they were safe. My wife and I could breathe again. But I had to keep my joy concealed from the officials who made frequent visits to the house to question me. They were eager to imprison the organizer so it was imperative that I keep my status as the boat owner hidden. Even without concrete evidence, they frequently threatened to arrest me. After about a year, as the investigation progressed, my wife and I felt we had no choice but to move to Saigon with the younger children. Saigon was a good hiding place but Phố, Phấn and Lan Phương could not attend school and we could not have a permanent home. My remaining small family moved numerous times, from place to place, to avoid being caught.

There is a Vietnamese proverb about fate: *Mưu Sự Tại Nhân Thành Sự Tại Thiên.* A man can carry out his plan, but God has the final say. Once again, I faced a life-and-death decision. Before we left Đà Lạt, we received the sponsorship papers the children had sent from Canada. However, the ongoing investigation and our current illegal status meant I could not submit them to the government. Perhaps we should wait and hope that the regime eventually forgot about us. Perhaps, if I were very careful, I could eventually find the right officials to bribe. We still had the gold I had held in reserve in case I needed to bail the older children out of prison, so we could survive a while longer. But the gold would not last forever and there was no predicting how long the wait might be. I could not work, and my children had no home, no access to education. I had secured a future for my older children and was desperate to do the same for the younger ones. I would be turning sixty, and I was becoming impatient.

My wife and I decided to use the last of our gold to try another escape. I already had many of the necessary contacts and the sponsorship papers that were useless in Vietnam would be highly valuable in a refugee camp.

To avoid the prying eyes of the communist officials, my wife remained in Saigon with Phổ, Phấn and Lan Phương while I made a secret trip to Đà Lạt to pay a last visit to Mỹ Phương and her family. Once again, they had chosen to stay behind and would continue to live in our home. It began to rain heavily as I arrived back in Đà Lạt and started walking home. A few years earlier, I would have walked in the pouring rain. This time I preferred to wait and decided to take refuge at Linh Sơn Temple. I lit incense and knelt in the main hall to pray to Buddha. The head monk chanted a Buddhist mantra and prayed with me. We prayed in silence, he for peace and me for wisdom. Had I made the right decision or should I wait for the right time to come and leave Vietnam legally?

Afterward, the monk offered me some tea and, strangely, also offered me extra, private prayers. I wondered if he sensed a fatal event was about to unfold. I took it as an omen that my time on earth was nearing its end but still wanted to proceed with my decision, to do the best I could for my family. That evening, I cuddled my three grandchildren for the last time.

The day before I died, we left Saigon for Bà Rịa, Vũng Tàu, retracing the steps I believed my other children had taken two years ago. We were directed to hide in a poultry barn and wait until it was dark. When night came, a *đề lô* arrived and guided us through bushes and past small farmhouses as the sound of barking dogs echoed through the fields. Along the way, many other groups of escapees gathered to walk the same path. Suddenly, we heard a scream and people started running. I led my family to a big willow tree where we hid with a few other escapees. We heard gunshots in the distance. Lan Phương cried silently when fire ants began to bite; my wife tried to comfort her while the other escapees signalled that she had to stay completely quiet.

I felt a strange foreboding, an intuition that something was wrong. I could not control what was coming next and considered taking my family back to Saigon. But I could not control our situation there either. I felt vulnerable and confused and acted on instinct. We kept following the other escapees, running after the *đề lô* when we were told it was safe.

We were instructed to run through vast fields of mud to get to the small boats that would take us to a bigger boat near the ocean. I thought of my six older children running through these same fields two years before. Phấn had tied his shoes too tight, now his feet were heavy with mud. I used both my lighter and cigarettes to burn his shoelaces and free his feet.

We finally arrived at the riverbank and walked through shallow water to get to the waiting canoes and water taxis. The escape boat was overcrowded with more than two hundred people fighting for space. But it was too late for me to take my family back to land. No one was allowed to leave in case they notified the authorities.

The boat departed at dawn. The engine started, but the boat moved slowly, unable to gain speed. It turned out that, amidst the chaos, no one had raised the anchor. The boat dragged it a short distance until the rope broke. The overcrowded boat moved on, but the anchor stayed behind, buried in the riverbed. Many people were upset; everyone knew a boat without its anchor would not be able to complete its journey. It was a bad omen.

By late afternoon, the boat still had not reached the safety of international waters. As the sky darkened, a pod of dolphins suddenly appeared and began swimming alongside the boat. It was another bad omen—dolphins were believed to be driven by the spirits of escapees who'd drowned and wanted to pull the boat down under the waves to join them. Many people started to chant their prayers; my wife lit incense and prayed with the children. We were all relieved when the dolphins dove under the water and the fearful sight of them was gone.

The sky suddenly turned black, covered by a thick dark cloud, signalling an approaching storm. The boat stalled, its propeller caught in a fishing net. The captain tried to maneuver away but lost control because of the excessive weight and the strong waves. The boat began moving in a circle, becoming more and more entangled. The fish in the net died, and their bloody bodies also began to circle the boat. The dolphins appeared again to feast on the dead fish. The atmosphere became eerie as people started to scream, begging and praying for the boat to stop.

The fishermen's boat appeared on the horizon and quickly caught up to us. They were friendly at first but got angry when they saw their net and discovered that their catch had been destroyed. They threw ropes, tied our boat to theirs, and pulled, intending to save their net from being further damaged. Many escapees became even more agitated, their screams adding to the chaos. The fishermen became angrier and used their radio to contact a police boat, which soon appeared in the distance.

The fishermen started to argue amongst themselves and finally decided to cut the ropes and drove away. The moment they cut the lines, our boat became unbalanced and tilted to one side. I looked into the wheelhouse and found it empty. The captain had already jumped into the ocean to avoid being captured. There was no one controlling the boat.

The police fired a few warning shots. People fought frantically among themselves for life jackets, cursing and jumping into the ocean. The boat listed more and more. Women, men and children screamed, their cries mixing with the high-pitched, harsh-edged squeaky sound of the dolphins. Death had arrived and was sucking the fear out of every human. The fishing boat saw the escape boat slowly sinking and turned back to the rescue.

I gathered my crying wife and children to me. My chest started to hurt; my working eye started to see double. I tried to remain calm and managed to get hold of a single life jacket. I had no choice—I tied the life jacket to my two sons and told them to jump. "I am very sorry. Stop crying and save yourselves. Remember to stick together! Close your eyes and jump quickly. Please, sons, listen to me. Jump and keep on swimming to that fishing boat."

They were so scared. They trembled, their bodies shaking in distress. They cried louder and did not move an inch. I finally picked both of them up and threw them into the ocean.

The boat tilted even more and began to fill with seawater, sinking faster. My panic increased, but I caught a glimpse of my two young sons moving in the water. I held both my daughter and my wife tightly but did not know what to do next. Then the boat made a cracking sound and flipped.

We all fell into the water. I lost control of my arms and felt Lan

Phương slip away from me. My wife was clinging to the boat. I grabbed a broken board and managed to hold on to her. She did not know how to swim so I tried to kick my legs to keep her head above water. I called out for my daughter, swallowing seawater as I screamed her name. My chest hurt and my energy was fading. From a distance, I heard her calling and crying out for me—her father—and saw the blurry image of her small hands reaching for me. Then they disappeared.

Oh God, what had I done? My chest hurt again. I felt a sharp pain in my heart. I gathered all my remaining strength and pushed my wife a short distance along the waves toward the fishing boat. My whole body became stiff. I could not swim or move anymore. My mouth filled with salty, bloody water. Everything started to turn black. I tried but I could not breathe; the oxygen refused to enter my lungs. I lost the remaining vision in my only functional eye and everything went completely black. Then, suddenly, I felt so light. I could see again and I felt that I could fly. I saw the light, and I saw God at the Door of Heaven.

CHAPTER 24

THE TEARS OF HEAVEN

It was raining hard on that day near the end of June, the sky unusually dark for a hot summer day in Canada. Fierce winds beat the heavy rain, the tears of Heaven, against the windows; thunder shook the old roof, trying to shatter it. The ringing phone had to compete with the sounds of the storm. It rang endlessly, shrill and insistent, until Hằng Phương finally picked up the receiver. Then she dropped it with an awful cry.

Death had arrived with that phone call and delivered its news without mercy—Father had died while trying to rescue Mother. Lan Phương had drowned, perhaps trapped inside a capsized boat. Her body had not been found. Mother, Phổ and Phấn were imprisoned at Côn Sơn Island. Father's body had been brought to Côn Sơn Island by the police boat; Mother had buried him on the beach.

I slumped to my knees, fighting for breath, my tears mingling with the pouring rain on my face. There was a sudden sharp pain near my heart as half my soul was ripped away. From that day on, all our hearts were broken.

Father's last letter was dated May 14, 1985. But it didn't reach Hamilton until a few months after he and Lan Phương died.

Saigon, May 14, 1985
Dearest Children,

. . . I miss you all very much. No words can describe how much we miss all of you. Your Mother, Phổ, Phấn, Lan Phương and I long to hear your voices. Your Mother and I miss the nights when we all sat together at the dinner table, all of you studying and completing your homework. Did you know that I watched you concentrate diligently on the task and I felt so proud? Your mother and I embedded in all of you the well-taught discipline that is the catalyst for determination and success. Your mother and I are confident that you will all become responsible citizens in the new country. Family is all about unconditional love for each other, always be there for each other, sharing happy times and achievements, and providing support during hardship.

I always thought I should always be there for you, even if you have matured. The parting from all of you is only temporary. We will reunite sooner than you have thought and anticipated. I long to hold each of you in my arms. Your mother expresses that she misses you all every single day, every single moment. Not a moment passes by that your mother, Phổ, Phấn, Lan Phương and I are not thinking about all of you. We miss hearing your laughter. We want to hear all about the hardship that you have been through. You must have been working very hard, in order to obtain the sponsorship approval paper for us. I am holding onto the paper and keeping it safe. Keep in mind, working in the factories is temporary, try to save enough money to live on and go back to school. Education is the foundation for your life and the key for your success.

You will find another address to send a letter back to us. I write it at the end of the letter. Hopefully, this letter will get to you. Perhaps, this letter will arrive in Canada after you hear good news from us. Perhaps, the day that I can sit on the porch to drink a Canadian beer with my sons is within our reach . . .

I am writing this letter while your mother, Phố, Phấn and Lan Phương are asleep. This is another temporary small place that we are renting and recently moved into. This current life of moving from place to place is not good for Phố, Phấn and Lan Phương. I watch them sleep and feel anxious and worried. I start to feel that I am old and weary. I am turning sixty soon, I feel impatient, like I am running against time.

Love you all.

Your Father

Lan Phương died on June 15, 1985, her ninth birthday.

Dearest Lan Phương,

I wish I could fly away with my soul in the form of a ghost. Death could come and take me for just a few days. I would be able to communicate with the spirits in the world of the dead and search for your body. Our souls could embrace.

I hope—unreasonably, I know—that your body is buried on land, in an unknown grave somewhere on Côn Sơn Island. I have also often dreamed that you were rescued, alive and adopted. You do not remember us for some reason, but you would recognize me if I found you. Lan Phương, I keep imagining how you would grow up, having your own family, our children playing happily together.

Every year, instead of celebrating our birthdays together, I will light incense to remember your death. I am overwhelmed with sorrow every time I see an orchid, every time I remember your voice singing "When the Last Leaf Falls," every time I play the guitar. The notes are so empty without your singing and without Father's interpretating the hidden meaning behind each verse.

I wish God would let me go back in time. I would persuade our parents to allow you to escape with me. I did not have the courage back then to speak my mind, burdened by the tradition of absolute obedience. This would be the best promise I ever made to Mother and Father, to make them believe and change their minds. After all, we two sisters used to do everything together. I could take care of you as I did when you were a baby. I would carry you on my back like I usually did on my way to school. I would protect you fiercely and we would safely flee Vietnam together. We would remember and search for the mermaids together.

Heaven has foreshadowed our fate. June is a month of loss, of sad memories and of restless souls. You have no grave, no decorated tombstone. There is no peaceful resting place for me to visit and bring your favourite flowers. Instead, your grave is the vast ocean, its salty water cruelly dissolving your flesh. Where can I find you? Are there any spirits out there who could help me search for you, in my desperate grief? Or must I imagine your spirit is present in the white foam formed by the tide, like the mermaid in Hans Christian Andersen's fairy tale, heartbroken and weeping for a short life and a tragic death.

Two sisters, ten years apart, both born in June, both quick to cry when displeased about something. Now, one has stopped crying, the other has started crying forever.

Dearest Lan Phương,
I love you.
Let us reunite in daily dreams.
I forever miss you.
Let us be sisters in our souls.
Forever together in this life . . .
Again . . . into our next life.

CHAPTER 25

THE BUTTERFLIES

Many more escapees were captured near the island and transported to Côn Sơn prison. The government quickly ran out of holding cells and instructed the warden to release the children and families of sick prisoners. Three months after the fateful day in June, my wife, Phổ and Phấn were released from Côn Sơn Prison due to her deteriorating health. The smile I had fallen in love with had left her face, forever buried with my corpse. The ship carried them away from the island, officially freeing them from detention, but their souls remained imprisoned by grief.

They were back to Đà Lạt under house restrictions, monitored by the local officials. Phổ and Phấn were given permission to enroll back in school but the family was only allowed occasional visits from close relatives. Our home became another prison, one filled with depression and anguish. On the first day of her return, my wife lit incense on the altar and whispered her prayer. "Dear husband and Lan Phương, we are back in the comfort of our home. Every single spot in the house reminds me of the touch of you and the laugh of Lan Phương."

My wife again faced a dreadful time with the communist government. The photos of my body taken on Côn Sơn Island were brought to Đà Lạt and posted at the central police station as a warning to other citizens thinking of trying to escape their homeland.

A policeman paid an unannounced visit to the house to criticize and condemn the family's sin—the sin of escaping the country; he maintained Lan Phương and I had deserved to die. My wife had to bribe him to leave the house. So my death was both exposed and extorted.

My soul lingered in our home and I became even more concerned for my wife. She rarely smiled or cried. She had become like a cactus —a plant whose leaves have evolved into spines to adapt to a harsh environment. She had been through so much suffering, both mentally and physically, and had adapted to live on. She appeared cold and prickly on the outside, but inside she was full of the tears she was holding in.

I longed to hear the temple bell ring; the daily sound of the mantra attracted my soul to Linh Sơn Temple. The night before the one-hundredth-day ritual that would mark the end of mourning, I chose to pray at the temple while my wife, Phổ and Phấn prayed in front of the altar,

"Father, you are here to pray too."

"Lan Phương!"

We hugged each other.

Lan Phương gave me her usual gentle smile. "Father, I am so happy to see you here."

"I am so happy to see you as well. It has been three months since you disappeared."

"Death came to collect my soul. It was so sudden."

"I did not see Death."

"You could not see Death because God granted your request to remain on earth."

"Why are you still here?" I worried Lan Phương had chosen the same path as mine.

"I told Death I needed more time to look for my body."

"Have you found it?"

"No. I think it is still floating somewhere in the Pacific Ocean."

"How long do you have?"

"I have until after the one-hundredth-day ritual."

"That is tomorrow." I had no tears to shed.

"Do you want to prove to the living that we are with them? I figured out how to do it." Lan Phương was proud of herself.

"Yes, Lan Phương. I really want to."

"We will borrow the butterfly's wings. Chị Jolie and I used to play our make-believe games near the flower bed surrounding the temple bell tower. We imitated the butterflies, imagining we could fly. Sometimes we chased them too. Yesterday, I played there. I chased one white butterfly. I found my soul could stay on its wings and I could fly like one of them. I thanked the butterfly and asked if it could fly to our house, and it did. We can both do that tomorrow."

"The wind must be calm with no rain. And we have to make sure that the butterfly does not get hurt," I reminded Lan Phương.

"Yes, Father. We will be careful. You have to try to chase one too." Her face was full of excitement. "The butterflies start to gather at the flower bed after the fog dissipates. They are most active in the early afternoon, under the sunlight. We will go to find them after the one-hundredth-day ceremony."

The next morning, our home's steel front doors were wide open to allow access for the dead. My two younger sisters, Hiển and Tánh, were allowed a rare visit to perform the ceremony with the rest of my family. They brought vegan food and my wife prepared a tofu dish. Flowers, fruit, mung bean cakes and vegan dishes were placed on the altar as an offering. A monk from Linh Sơn Temple came to the house and chanted a Buddhist mantra to soothe both the dead and the living. Lan Phương was trying to hug her mother, Phổ, Phấn, Mỹ Phương and her family. I sat and watched the incense burn: would this ritual would truly end their sorrow?

After the ceremony was completed, my wife and sisters gathered to have tea and comfort each other.

"We did not hear about their deaths until two weeks after the tragedy. Lan Phương was so young and beautiful. Poor soul! And Anh Hiên, buried on that isolated island…!" Hiển referred to me by my nickname.

"The news did not get to us until a ship brought some prisoners from other failed escapees to Saigon from Côn Sơn Island." Tánh added in tears. "Someone from the boat managed to send a message to Chú Tư's wife, who sent a telegram to Mỹ Phương, and she informed us."

"Every time I think about my dear brother's corpse buried on that island, in such an isolated place, far away from the rest of us, my heart saddens." Hiển's voice broke. "I feel so sorry for the children in Canada. And for Chú Tư, who had to call and deliver such terrible news."

"I don't know how my children in Canada took the news. Chú Tư called them again and told them we had been released. I need to write to them, to tell them what happened, but it is so painful to think about and write on paper. I must pull myself together to write a letter." My wife was struggling to hold back tears.

"Try to write to them soon," said Tánh.

"How were they doing for the past year, before your escape?" asked Hiển in a calmer voice.

"My children worked hard to earn enough money to support themselves and managed to continue their education. They live frugally to be able to send money back to help us."

"Anh Hiên held a full tiger birth sign. He was an extraordinary man. His courage will make his spirit a powerful one," said Tánh proudly.

The three women hugged each other, taking turns wiping tears from each other's cheeks.

"This ritual is for the ending of tears. Yet here we are, all of us are crying," said my wife.

Lan Phương came over to me. "Father, I think it is time to go back to the temple and find the butterflies."

She held my hand. "After the incense stops burning, I think Mother will still chat with Aunt Hiền and Aunt Tánh for a while. We will show them our existence. I will show you how."

We arrived at the flower bed surrounding the temple bell tower. The sun was shining and the gentle breeze favoured our mission.

"I found the same butterfly." The white, vibrant butterfly seemed to recognize Lan Phương and flapped its wings gently. "Father, find yours and chase it." The others sensed the disturbance and dispersed, all except for a grey butterfly with small rips on its wings. It stayed on the yellow marigold flowers before slowly flying away. I chased after it and found my soul could fly with it.

"Follow me Father, I will tell it what to do, your grey butterfly will be right beside mine." Lan Phương gave specific instructions to the butterflies who flew to our house, our souls on their wings.

My wife, Hiền and Tánh stopped talking as they watched us fly inside the house and hover around them.

"Father, do you want to hug Mother?"

"Yes, Lan Phương. I have done so many times, but I don't think she can feel it."

"This time, she will definitely know." Lan Phương instructed the grey butterfly to land on my wife's nose as I wrapped my arms around her. I felt that she sensed my touch. The white butterfly flapped its wings vigorously around the grey one, as Lan Phương encouraged the grey butterfly to linger. I wanted to hold on to this moment a bit longer, but we knew it had to end.

Lan Phương and I whispered our thanks to the grey butterfly.

It flapped its ripped wings to fly outside, followed by its white companion.

Hiền cried out loud, her voice trembling. "Anh Hiên misses you. The grey butterfly must be him. He just kissed you on your nose!"

Tánh sobbed louder. Her hand reached for her sister-in-law. "Lan Phương is the white butterfly that danced around both of you!"

My wife sat still, speechless.

The end of the one hundredth day was near. Lan Phương wanted to be at the temple when Death came for her.

"Father, this is my favourite place. One time, Chị Jolie brought the guitar here. We pretended that the butterflies were our audience. We sang most of the songs we knew to entertain them."

"Lan Phương, can you sing a song for me? One last time."

She sang "When the Last Leaf Falls," and her voice was as sweet as ever. I could not cry. The day I failed to save her was the day I shed my last tear.

Should I negotiate with Death to let Lan Phương stay with me a few days longer? But there was no rain, no fierce wind and no forlorn tree. I held her hands tightly, loathe to let go.

Lan Phương reassured me, "I am not scared of Death."

She gave me her warmest smile, "Dearest Father, I loved you in life and in death."

Her voice was more peaceful than ever. "Death will guide me to Heaven."

My wife knew something was wrong inside her body, but an intelligent person can become thoughtless in the presence of regret and fear. Her uterus had nurtured twelve children as a testament to the love we shared for almost thirty years. Now that love had been replaced by sorrow, it was slowly growing deadly tumours.

I was desperate to find a way to help her and spent my days pacing back and forth on our flat aluminum roof, a place where I could think without distraction. I believed only I could hear my footsteps, but my wife did too.

During dinner one night, she questioned Phổ and Phấn. "I've been hearing footsteps on the roof for the past few days. Did either of you hear that? Or did you walk on the roof?"

"I don't think I heard anything," Phấn answered, looking at Phổ.

"Me neither, Mother. I did not walk on the roof at all. Did you, Phấn?"

"No, I didn't."

"When you hear the noise again, let me know. I will climb up onto the roof and check for you," Phổ reassured his mother.

The next day, I stomped my feet to make a louder noise. Then I stood still and watched my wife climb the ladder at the back of the house to check if anyone was on the roof. She went back down the ladder and walked over to the neighbour's house.

"Did you hear any noises on our roof lately?" she asked Mrs. Nguyễn.

"No, I didn't hear anything but I will check, just to make sure there aren't any robbers." Mrs. Nguyễn was concerned for my wife.

"It is bizarre. I heard the noises, then climbed onto the roof to check immediately, but I saw no one. I'm sure no one could vanish from such a big area in just a few seconds."

My wife sensed my presence; I wanted to demonstrate that I remained with her, providing what comfort I could. On the nights without electricity, Phổ and Phấn prepared and lit the oil lamps and each carried one around the house. But when my wife moved hers, I blew out the flame. She re-lit the lamp; again I extinguished the flame. Finally, she stopped using the oil lamp and settled in the dark, knowing that I was trying to console her.

My sons did not vocalize their grief, but I knew they were

heartbroken, just like their mother. They focused on their studies as I had taught them. At night, I sat by their beds and watched them sleep just as I used to do with their siblings. I was used to the fact that they did not feel me but still I kissed their foreheads and wrapped myself around them. One night I was caressing Phở's hair, smoothing away the loose strands that hung across his eyes, when he suddenly reached out and grabbed my arm. He could feel me, but not see me and he sat up, wholly awake and starting to sweat.

The following day, I heard him ask his brother, "Did you feel anything strange last night? I felt someone caressing my hair. I reached out my hands and it seemed that I touched someone's arm."

Phấn was not surprised. "It must have been Father. I feel his presence in the house. Do you?"

"I think so too. But it was too dark, pitch black. I wish I could see Father for real."

More than half a year passed, a short time that felt like a century for both the living and the dead. Time muted some of the emotional pain but my wife's physical pain worsened. I decided to take a trip to Mũi Né. Perhaps I could do something to make my brother-in-law Phát come to Đà Lạt and convince his sister to see to her health.

Mũi Né is famous for its vast sand dunes and forests of palm trees that stretch along the shoreline. We had often vacationed here, our children running free and counting their footsteps in the white sand. Now my footprints left no trace. We had buried my wife's parents in one of the cemeteries nested in the sand dunes and I lingered around their graves, thinking of mine on Côn Sơn Island, without a tombstone.

I proceeded to Phát's house, located right next to the beach, the sound of the waves dictating the natural rhythm of family life. He had carried on his parents' business and operated a photo studio in his home. I hoped that, at some point, he would feel my presence. At night, when he lit incense and prayed, I sat beside him, praying to the Bodhisattva of Compassion to work her miracle. The following day, when he visited his parents' graves, I was right next to him.

When he returned, he talked to his wife. "I plan to take the bus to Đà Lạt tomorrow."

"I thought you planned to do so next month."

"For the past few days, I have felt uneasy. I feel the presence of my brother-in-law and keep thinking of Chị Hai. For three consecutive nights, I have dreamed of him and of taking Chị Hai to the hospital in Saigon."

"But you may get into trouble."

"I know the right people to bribe so they will leave us alone."

The following day, he left for Đà Lạt. He arrived to find a grieving widow who swallowed sorrow as if it was food, hoping it would be fully digested and no longer hurt.

"Why did you take such a huge risk to come visit me?" asked my wife, even though she knew the question would hurt his feelings.

"Chị Hai, please, do not worry," he replied, addressing her by her pet name. "I already bribed the local officials. I made sure that my visit was allowed before I came here."

"Bribery may add another conviction to my record," my wife said bitterly.

"I should have come sooner. I think I waited too long." He hesitated for a second, then asked cautiously, "Are you sick right now? You are a nurse. You know very well if your body has something bad going on inside it."

"How do you know I am sick?" His sister became irritated.

"I knew it! Listen to me, Chị Hai, please. Let me explain." After taking a deep breath, he continued. "In a dream, I brought you to a hospital in Saigon. But before that dream, I saw brother-in-law, your husband, but not at my house. I saw him walking on the roof of your house."

My wife paid close attention to Phát's words but did not answer. She had hidden her illness from everyone.

Phát continued to be patient with her. "Chị Hai, you must take care of your health. I think you have been sick since you were released from the prison in Côn Sơn. You are saying nothing, but I know from the dream and from my gut."

"I know something is horribly wrong, but I have no energy left to do anything." My wife finally uttered the truth.

"From what I saw in my dream, brother-in-law wants me to take you to Saigon, to the hospital there, on my way back to Mũi Né." His tone was firm.

"Do you think I would be able to leave here? I doubt I still have any strength left to try."

Listening to their conversation, I wanted to show my presence, to tell my wife to look after her health. I climbed up to the roof and stomped my feet right above the kitchen where they sat.

My wife shivered and Phát, startled, stood up and yelled, "What was that? Who walks on the roof?" He ran through the back door and climbed up the ladder but of course there was no sign of any living creature.

Walking back into the kitchen, he understood. "Brother-in-law is sending you a message. He wants you to be healthy. You still have Phố and Phấn to care for, you must accompany them to Canada. You need to reunite with your six older children and find a way for Mỹ Phương and her family to join them in Canada as well. I think brother-in-law is not happy that you are neglecting your health."

My wife listened without saying a word.

Phát continued, "Besides, you need to think about bringing his remains back from the island, to Đà Lạt or to Huế. You need to be healthy to achieve that. Côn Sơn is not where he wanted to be buried."

"But my movements are restricted," said his sister, still full of negativity.

"Your health is a priority. It is a sensible reason for them to lift the restriction."

A few days later, Phát bribed the officials to release my wife from the order limiting her movements. She could leave Đà Lạt for surgery. Early on a foggy morning, they boarded a bus to Saigon. As soon as they arrived, my wife checked herself into the hospital and, the very next day, underwent an operation for a hysterectomy while Phát and Khoa, her other brother who lived in Saigon, waited outside the operating room. I was with her the entire time, holding her hands while she was put under general anesthesia. The doctor informed them that the deadly tumours in her uterus were removed just in time.

After she was discharged, my wife stayed in Saigon, at the home of Chú Tư, whose wife and two younger daughters had stayed behind in Saigon. Thím Tư nursed her back to health. As my wife began to recover physically and emotionally, she confided to her brother about a dream. "My husband came to visit me in the hospital while I was in the recovery unit."

Phát listened attentively.

"But it was strange because he said nothing. He just looked at me, not smiling at all. I saw his sad eye, without his usual dark sunglasses." My wife's eyes looked into empty space.

Phát began to cry as he imagined his brother-in-law losing his sunglasses in the sea, struggling in the waves trying to rescue his daughter.

"He looked worried. I know that look. I keep thinking about it. While he said nothing, he was wearing a raincoat made of palm leaves and woven grass, not the nylon kind we wore in Đà Lạt. Even so, his body was soaked and dripping with seawater." Her words brought more tears to Phát's eyes.

"Chị Hai, he was trying to tell you that he wants to get off Côn Sơn Island. You have to act quickly. If another big storm passes through, his shallow grave could be washed into the sea."

CHAPTER 26

MY SECOND FUNERAL

My body had rested below that field of grass on Côn Sơn Island for more than a year by the time Khoa was able to bribe the right individuals.

"Khoa and I have handed your gold to officials who take frequent trips to Côn Sơn Island by helicopter. You and one other person can accompany them the next time the helicopter is flying there. No one wants a corpse on a boat." Phát explained.

A few weeks later, my wife received a letter from her niece, Mai, who lived in Đà Lạt, urgently asking for a meeting. When she returned to Đà Lạt to prepare for the trip to Côn Sơn Island, she met with Mai at her house.

The minute she stepped through the door, Mai pointed to a chair in a living room. "Aunty, I must tell you: I saw Uncle sitting right on this chair, soaking wet and very sad," she said, wiping away tears. It had been a rainy day when I visited Mai's house.

"Uncle is giving a sign that he does not want to be alone on that island. My husband wants to go with you to Côn Sơn, to help bring him back." Her cry was louder.

When Mai's husband, Thiện, had been sent to a political re-education camp, I had helped care for her family. I knew Thiện would want to repay my kindness.

When my wife was finally able to return to Côn Sơn Island with

185

Thiện, they weren't able to find my grave. She was stunned by the size of the field that now covered the beach, nature unfettered. They could not do anything in the short time the helicopter pilot allowed them. They were forced to wait in Saigon until they could arrange a full-day trip by helicopter.

The second time, the helicopter dropped them off in the early morning. The sky was clear, the island bright with sunshine as they searched the tall grass to find the circle of stones that marked my burial site. After hours of searching, they still could not locate it. I was watching their every move, yet I could not express how happy I was to see them, but could not direct them to my grave.

Around noon, Thiện lit some incense and called out to me in frustration, his voice echoing off the mountains on this deserted part of the island. He and my wife knelt and prayed, each with bunch of incense between their fingers. Afterward, they walked slowly, randomly placing the incense on different part of the grounds, struggling to evoke their sixth sense. I yearned for them to feel my spirit as much as they did. The earnestness of both the living and the dead pushed against the barrier between them. Finally, Thiện called out that he had found the exact location of my burial site. He later told Mai that he felt my spirit around him, guiding him.

Thiện traced the pattern of the stones and cut back the grass to investigate. He began to dig, his heart racing, his sweat mingling with tears as chills ran down his spine, despite the heat and his exertion. When he reached my bones, my wife asked him to check under my feet. The moment they found the black plastic bag, she knew for sure it was me. She wept when she recognized the clothes that I had been wearing. What remained of my light blue shirt and black pants were now loosely mixed with dirt, sand and bones.

Thiện carefully picked up every single bone and placed it in a small wooden coffin. He started with my skull and moved systematically toward my feet. As a nurse, my wife knew the order of the bones and which would stay intact, and she made sure they didn't miss any. Thiện worked non-stop, anxious to finish the task before the helicopter pilot lost patience, especially as a storm was approaching.

When most of my bones had been collected, a sudden, torrential rain soaked the land. The toe bones, the only ones remaining, were quickly buried in muddy water. Thiện thrust his hand through the pool of water and dirt but could not feel them. They were too small and seemed to be hiding from him. He and my wife had to stop and hurry back to the helicopter.

I did not mind the absence of my toe bones in my coffin. I was grateful that my wife had found my body and arranged to bring my remains to Đà Lạt. I decided that my toe bones could remain as a testament to my adventurous spirit and the significant time I had spent on this island. A week later, a tropical storm wiped out the beach on Côn Sơn.

When they returned to Saigon, my wife and Thiện brought my coffin to a cremation centre so that my bones could be completely dried and disinfected. Then she secretly placed them into a small travel bag for the bus trip back to Đà Lạt. People are very superstitious and would not want the dead travelling with them. Thiện carried the travel bag on his shoulder, respectfully whispering my name intermittently. My wife held tight to the travel bag throughout the journey, hugging my remains.

They parted ways at the main bus station in Đà Lạt. My wife went straight to the Linh Sơn Temple where she arranged with the head monk to have my bones placed in the morgue, a separate building used to house dead bodies before a funeral. The head monk remembered my last visit.

"Your husband and I had tea for the last time when he took refuge from the rain, over a year ago. I knew him. You should find the right spot for him at Du Sinh Cemetery. Where he is buried is very important for him." He lit some incense then continued. "You need to obtain a permit to get a spot at Du Sinh Cemetery, the new burial site recently created by the communist government. While you are doing that, your husband's remains will be prepared properly."

"How will I know that I picked the right burial spot at the cemetery?"

The monk paused briefly. "There is an ascetic monk who is considered a master in reading a person's past life. Many people trust him to choose the correct and suitable spot."

He handed my wife a piece of paper. "The government is currently monitoring his whereabouts and actions due to his ties with the previous government. He was just released from a political re-education camp. Here is the address near Du Sinh Cemetery where he stays. Give him this note, so he knows that I send you."

At the morgue, my bones were once again exposed to the air as the head monk conscientiously took them out of the travel bag and wrapped them in a red cloth. He placed a white band around the forehead of my skull so that, when her time came, I could mourn my mother's death as a dutiful son.

He lit incense and chanted Buddhist scriptures for three days, praying for my soul to be free from this earth. He did not know that I had defied the process. I could not leave the living world; I still had so much left undone. I needed to reunite the family and I wanted to see Canada and America. I would remain between life and death.

When my wife met with the ascetic monk, his first sentence caused her to tremble with fear. "Your husband is sitting right beside you now." Adding to her dismay, he shared a fact known solely to her and Thiện. "Your husband expresses his gratitude that his bones have been brought back to this land. His toe bones remain on Côn Sơn Island, and it is meant to be so."

He then slowly walked up the steepest of the hills that make up Du Sinh Cemetery, carrying burning incense in his hands, my wife following. He stopped at the spot near the top, turned around to look down the hill, kowtowed in six directions—up toward the sky and down toward the earth, then east, south, west and north—then finally stuck the incense in the chosen burial spot.

"The day of his burial, I will be here to perform a final inspection, to ensure that all the bones are arranged in proper order. When the cemetery workers lower the coffin into the ground, they must do so carefully to avoid disturbing them."

Funeral possessions often used to pass in front of our house on the way to Linh Sơn Temple. The mourners walked behind a slow-moving funeral car designed to carry the coffin. The music, the Buddhist mantras, and the sound of the funeral drum filled the road. People and children came out of their houses to watch. Some prayed for the dead.

For my second funeral, there were no funeral marches, no crowd of mourning children and relatives walking behind the decorated funeral car, no first-born child carrying my framed image. Instead, my remains were secretly transported to Du Sinh Cemetery in a three-wheeled Lambro. A rectangular wooden coffin, just large enough for my bones, was positioned between the two rows of passenger seats, empty except for my wife, alone again. Black clouds covered the entire sky, then Heaven cried as the front wheel of the Lambro sliced through the stream of water and fought the flooded roads. The engine forced the three wheels up the muddy hill, trying to reach the grave that had been dug the day before. But the hill was too steep and the mud made it slippery. Nature forced the Lambro to stop at the bottom of the hill, where Phổ, my son-in-law Kim, my younger sisters Hiến and Tánh, and the ascetic monk were patiently waiting for my arrival.

In the pouring rain, Phổ and Kim led the procession up the hill, carefully carrying my coffin. My sisters, wife and the ascetic monk followed. The workers used buckets to drain the hole and waited until dusk for the rains to lessen. The monk performed the last prayer and inspected the coffin to ensure the movement had not disturbed the arrangement of my bones. The workers secured the lid of the coffin, sealing my bones from the air, and then lowered it into the muddy soil under the watchful eye of the monk, who left immediately afterward in case any officials have braved the rain.

Phấn, as the youngest child, remained at home to avoid being pulled into the world of the dead. Mỹ Phương stayed home to take care of her three young children. The chief monk from Linh Sơn temple came to the house, chanted Buddhist scriptures and lit incense on my altar while the burial took place at the cemetery.

Early the next morning, Phổ and Phấn rode their bicycles to Du Sinh Cemetery with their mother. Standing beside my new grave, they wept more, and my wife wept less.

My children in Canada knew nothing of my second funeral until, several weeks later, they received a letter from their mother. She explained that, if she had arrived a week later, my grave would have been washed to sea by a tropical storm that had wiped out the beach on Côn Sơn Island. She included a photo of her kneeling beside a rectangular wooden box with Thiện standing nearby holding a shovel. Another photo showed Phổ and Kim carrying my coffin up the hill. The last was of Phấn and Mỹ Phương's children, white funeral bands tied across their foreheads, standing by the altar behind a monk who was securing sticks of incense into the brass burner. There, beside the statue of Buddha, stood framed photos of me and Lan Phương.

CHAPTER 27

PARALLEL WORLDS

As soon as I arrived in Đà Lạt, I began making arrangements to visit my father's grave. Two years before, Phú had returned to Vietnam; he had rebuilt the graves of Father, Hoàng Trọng Phụ, and those of our siblings, Hoàng Trọng Phu and Hoàng Thị Hồng Phương. In addition, he had erected a tombstone engraved with the name Hoàng Thị Lan Phương, entwined with lotuses, even though her body was not inside. The graves were cared for by a distant relative who I had hoped would escort me. I tried phoning him but there was no answer.

I arranged for the hotel driver to drive us to Du Sinh Cemetery in the morning, before the rain that comes almost every afternoon in June. The driver took us to Đà Lạt Supermarket where we bought flowers, incense and food to conduct a memorial service, and then to the cemetery itself. I kept calling my relative, but there was still no answer. When we arrived, I felt overwhelmed. Clusters of graves covered three hills. Looking up, I could see multiple layers of tombstones, white mixed with black, massive and tiny, thousands of them, crowded one on top of the another.

Phú had rebuilt the graves with rare black marble, unique among all the graves of Du Sinh Cemetery, but I had only a vague idea of where they were located. I vaguely remembered Mother told me to walk up the main path of the central hill, then turn right near the top of the slope. The driver drove me around to find the main hill and the main gate, but everywhere looked the same. He suggested I come back after I had contacted my relative but I was determined to find the grave. Stubbornly, I told the driver to wait for me at the bottom of the hill and, without any other plan, grabbed the hands of my daughters and started walking.

The weather seemed to cooperate with us as we walked up, down and around looking for the black marble grave. Still, we did not know where to turn, left or right. After more than an hour, we were completely lost. My daughters were scared; they had never seen so many graves, surrounded by pictures of the dead looking straight at them with gloomy eyes.

"Mommy, I'm scared. I want to go back to the hotel," said Như Thương, close to tears.

"Should we go back? Too many graves, Mommy!" Hoàng Thương said softly.

"Mom, I dropped my sunglasses somewhere," Diệu Thương told me.

I said nothing but spread my arms to hug my frightened daughters. "We will find the grave. I know it! It is just a matter of time. Your grandfather knows that we are looking for his resting place."

I closed my eyes and prayed aloud. "Dear Father, I am coming to visit you. I cannot wait any longer. Please guide me to the location of your grave."

I couldn't tell if my words comforted or frightened them. No one was around, not a single living person. I felt a cool breeze blowing my hair as I called out again. "Father, I know your spirit is here, around me, please guide me to your grave." I imagined the wind carrying my desperate voice to him.

A stronger gust suddenly blew across my face. Then I saw a woman in her fifties walking up the slope toward us. She stopped a short distance away.

Acting on instinct, I asked her, "Do you think you can help us find my father's grave?"

She stared at us in silence, her gaze sharp, her expression making my daughters tremble. Despite the cool breeze, I began to sweat.

I pulled myself together. "The name on the grave is Hoàng Trọng Phụ, and his Buddhist name is Tâm Bình."

"Is the grave made of black marble?"

"Yes!" my daughters and I yelled at once.

"Stand here, don't move or go anywhere. You will get lost again, and I won't be able to find you. Just wait right here," she said in a stern voice as she walked away.

"Is she going to help us, Mommy?"

"Is she going to come back, Mommy?"

"Do you think you can trust her, Mom?"

I did not know how to answer. I was asking myself the same questions. We stood where we were and waited.

A few minutes later, the woman was back. "Follow me!"

I wondered if I should trust her. Was I putting my daughters in some sort of danger? She kept walking, leading us further up, changing direction, turning left and right a few times. I recognized a path we had been on earlier. She abruptly turned around and asked us to wait as she turned to her right and walked down a narrow path between graves. Following her progress, I could see the black marble grave, standing out from the others, farther along the path. Now I recalled my mother saying the grave was located way up high on the hill. I had been close earlier but hadn't gone up far enough. I quickly led my daughters down the path.

Kneeling in front of my father's grave, the tears I had held inside for so many years were finally released. The dead and the living were so near but could not embrace. We were separated by a thick layer of dirt, shielded by the beautiful black marble. The reality of his death was finally right in front of me. I lost any sense of time. While I surrendered to my grief, the lady who had helped us instructed my daughters to place the food and flowers on the grave. With the assistance of a complete stranger, my daughters conducted the memorial for their grandfather. They lit incense and prayed, handing some to me so that I could pray with them. They cried along with their mother.

A few yards away, we also found the grave for my dead siblings, Phu, Hồng Phương and Lan Phương. My daughters conducted another memorial for their dead uncle and aunts, again lighting incense and kneeling. Staring at Lan Phương's empty grave, grief continued to overwhelm me. I closed my eyes and again felt a gentle breeze blow across my face, as if someone caressed my hair to soothe my pain.

I recalled the conversation I had with Father about the deaths of Phu and Hồng Phương. His voice echoed in my mind, teaching me the intricate concept of forgetting—continuing to love and honour, but burying our anguish in the face of unbearable grief.

The lady who helped us find the grave, who now seemed kind and gentle, reminded us that the weather might change, the rain could start at any moment. As we parted, she handed me a folded note. I opened it as the driver drove us back to the hotel. She had written her address and a command: You must meet me tonight at my place after the sun has set. Remember, it must be after sunset. Your father sends you a message through me. The note was signed Tám Anh.

Lady Tám Anh lived at the bottom of the hill of Du Sinh Cemetery in a tiny rundown hut, clumsily put together with pieces of wood, rusty metal and dirty plastic sheets attached to the wall of another house. Inside was a narrow bamboo bed and, right next to it, a small table with two attached chairs.

I was filled with anxious anticipation as she asked me to sit directly across from her. The table was so small that our knees touched. Our faces were just a few inches from one another, separated by a tiny oil lamp, its flame flickering back and forth. In this confined place, so close to each other, I could discreetly observe her. Her eye flashed with the piercing gaze that had given us a chill, as if she could read my thoughts; they were the eyes of a person who lived in between the worlds of the living and the dead. She wore multiple layers of clothes, at least two sweaters, perhaps to fight the chilliness of the night weather of Đà Lạt, and a black wool hat from which a few strands of the white hair emerged to hang loosely on her wrinkled face.

She started the conversation. "Your Father was here and told me to come up the hills to find you and your daughters, to help you find his grave. He said he is very pleased that you and your daughters visited his resting place."

I felt a chill. "Is my father beside me, around me?" I asked, my voice trembling.

"Earlier, at the grave. But not here. He is up the hill."

She again looked straight into my eyes. The wrinkles on her face seemed to deepen as she shook her head slightly, giving off the smell of unwashed sweat, a graveyard smell.

"Your sister's grave is empty." She closed her eyes briefly, then suddenly opened them wide as she shrieked, "Your father is tormenting himself with the thought that he could not save your sister!" Her voice dropped to a whisper. "I saw water surrounding her body."

My hands were shaking and my heart was beating fast. How could she know all that? I felt frightened, dizzy.

"Your house in Canada has plenty of big trees around it, but the roof needs to be fixed. Water will pour down into your home." This time her voice was calmer. "Your Father does not want to leave the living world. His spirit is around you, your mother and your siblings.

He travels between Vietnam, America and Canada, dividing his time among all of you, protecting his family."

How could she know that my house still had a leaky roof? That it was surrounded by trees? Lady Tám Anh seemed to be able to read my thoughts. She put her face near me, pressing her bony hand against mine hard enough to stop its trembling.

"The dead and the living coexist, side by side. You don't believe me?" Her voice was shrieking again even though she was trying to whisper.

I did believe her. I remembered how Father appeared in my dream, so clearly, smiling at me the night before I left for Vietnam. I felt comforted knowing that he was protecting his grandchildren and me while we were in Đà Lạt. When he had seen that my daughters and I were lost, frightened among the graves, he had asked lady Tám Anh to help us. I wanted to ask her more about Lan Phương, but my time was up.

"Leave now, I need to rest."

I hesitated, wanting to hear more, but she suddenly froze, then glared at me again. "Leave now, another person just arrived and wants to sit!"

There was no one around us. I felt goosebumps on my arms. Standing up, I almost fell out of the chair. I stepped out of the hut, sweating despite the cool evening air, my mind racing. I looked up the hill, in the direction of Father's grave, hoping I could catch a glimpse of him. It was dark and cold, but I felt a strange warmth soothing my heart.

A light flashed directly at me as the driver pulled the car up. As he drove me back to the hotel, he told me that Lady Tám Anh was famous for her gift of hearing and seeing ghosts. She slept during the day, almost never leaving her hut in the afternoon. She only ventured out at night to communicate with the dead and rarely let people into her hut, especially after sunset.

It was definitely not a coincidence. Even in death, my father loved his family and did what he could to protect us. I wished I could embrace him, tell him how much I missed him.

I thought of a mathematics professor I once had, lecturing on projective geometry. He wrote on the whiteboard, "Two parallel lines do not intersect in the real plane but intersect at a point in infinity."

Some of the students in the lecture hall gasped. Some whispered a complaint, "Oh gosh, another difficult theorem to prove."

The professor asked, "Can any of you think of a real-life example that demonstrates this proposition?"

No one answered.

"Try standing on a railroad. If you look down, you will see two parallel rails. But if you look further ahead, you will see that the two rails meet on the horizon.

The living cannot see the dead, but they can feel their aura. The dead and the living exist in two parallel worlds, lines running side by side, never meeting each other in this domain, but joining at a point in infinity.

I visited the cemetery every day of the week my daughters and I stayed in Đà Lạt. Once I lit a cigarette and placed it on top of Father's grave, remembering how he smoked whenever he was in a serious thinking mood. Father was the type of person who looked at a tree but saw the entire forest, someone who stood by the ocean knowing what he would find at the end of the horizon. His vision, courage and selflessness brought his children to freedom.

After each visit, I walked to Lady Tám Anh's place, but I never found her again.

CHAPTER 28

PIG BRAINS

We had a Vietnamese nickname for our guidance counsellor, Mr. Reed, one we never told him. We called him *Ông Tiên* meaning "kindest male fairy." His hair was silky white, his eyeglasses often hung on the tip of his nose, and every semester he used his magic pen to plot an educational map for each of us. He recommended that Phú participate in the computer programming club. He enrolled Phi in the chess club and put me in a woodwind band, playing the flute. He read the grades on our report cards with pride, then made extra copies, reminding us to send them to our parents.

After one year of working in the bakery, Phán quit his job and enrolled in Grade 13 to prepare for university, living off his savings. When Hằng Phương had saved enough money, she quit her job at the sewing factory and enrolled in Grade 12. A year later, she went on to study data processing at Mohawk College. Phiên also enrolled at Mohawk College in the Automotive Service Technician program. He and Thu Hà got married and moved to their own apartment while the rest of us remained in the townhouse. Mr. Reed was proud to have helped all five Hoàng siblings pursue post-secondary education.

Phán, Phú and I all earned top marks and received scholarships from a local business, Stelco-Dofasco, to attend university. The scholarships were enough for one year's tuition; after that, we would have to rely on the Ontario Student Assistance Program, student loans, co-op placements and a variety of part-time jobs. Phán was accepted to McMaster University for Mechanical Engineering the same year as Phú was accepted to the University of Waterloo for Computer Engineering. Phi followed Phú a year later to study Civil Engineering while I enrolled at McMaster with Phán. Mr. Reed personally delivered our university acceptance letters and scholarship certificates.

Unlike my siblings, I had a hard time choosing my career path and enrolled in sciences. Mother had hoped that my involvement with her business would encourage me to study medicine, but the truth was that my heart hurt before my brain had time to react to the sick and injured. I never wanted to disappoint her and often tried to think of a vague response while I hid her medicines in their secret spot.

Despite my dislike of blood, biology was one of my favourite subjects in high school. But after the deaths of Father and Lan Phương, as my brain began searching for the other half of my soul, I had a hard time memorizing complex biological terminology. It was mathematics that helped me focus whenever my mind became a chaotic tangle of endless unanswered questions. Pythagoras of Samos, besides famously determining that the square of the hypotenuse of a right triangle is equal to the sum of the squares of the other two sides, was a philosopher whose teaching held that, at its deepest level, reality is mathematical in nature. He identified the brain as the locus of the soul. I found his doctrine interesting and trained my mind to solve math problems, finding some comfort in understanding how numbers shape our lives.

Maintaining grades above 95 percent and winning scholarships did not guarantee our acceptance to university. The decisive factor was passing the Test of English as a Foreign Language (TOEFL), which evaluated reading, listening and writing. Phán and Phú got the required score on their second try but I was seven marks away from the target and had to take the test a third time. In June of 1987, Mr. Reed helped me prepare my identification: a landed immigrant document and a letter from the high school with a photo affixed and imprinted with the school seal.

Phán and Phú drove me to York University, two hours away, to take the exam. As I joined a long line of students, Phán wished me luck and reminded me to have my identification ready. Phú gave me a reassuring smile. "You will nail it this time, Jolie. Don't worry too much. I know you can do it." Then they left for another appointment.

I stood near the end of the line, holding my Grade 13 photo stamped with the high school emblem; above it was Mr. Reed's signature. The examination hall doors opened, and the proctors emerged to check everyone's identification. One of them, an older male Caucasian, began walking toward me, skipping everyone in line ahead of me. Without saying a word, he took the documents out of my hands, gave them a quick glance and returned them to me. Then he told me to step away from the line. Surprised and extremely confused, I stepped back in line and waited for my turn. When I got to the front, the same proctor said, "I already told you to step away from the line."

"I need to know why. I was waiting with my documents like everyone else."

"Your documents are not valid. You are not allowed to write the test."

"Can you explain why my documents are not valid?"

"Your documents are not valid because I said so. Step away from here and let everyone through."

My hand was shaking, and so was my voice. "My guidance counsellor helped me read the documentation requirements. This letter, with the school seal, over my photo, and his signature validates my identity. I have taken the same test before, using the same document. Why is it invalid this time?"

The proctor ignored me and none of his colleagues intervened, despite my entreaties. It was like I was not even there. The tall black double doors of the exam hall closed, leaving me alone in the hallway.

I started toward the pay phone then realized I had no idea where my brothers were and no way to reach them. I stepped outside and sat on the grass, alone with the sun and its heat. Four hours crawled past as I tried to understand human behaviour. When my brothers arrived, Phán marched into the building with my documents but the test was over; the proctor was nowhere to be found. After we returned home, Phú helped me register for the next available test. He also offered to drive me to work, but I was in a mood to walk.

Mary was ninety years old and my job was to care for her two nights per week. I slept in the bed opposite to hers and tended to her needs when she called me. She did not try to pronounce my Vietnamese name and called me "Fawn." I wasn't too fond of this name but did not object; it occurred to me that a little deer also falls a few times before it learns to stand.

I got this job because I could play the guitar and sing. Mary loved to hear me sing hymns and read her the Bible before bedtime. In the middle of the summer, she asked me to sing "Silent Night." Mary wanted to hear Vietnamese songs too. She enjoyed the melancholy sound without the burden of understanding lyrics that were even sadder. She loved it when I combed her hair as I had once combed my grandmother's.

Mary often enjoyed hearing about my day at school, but I didn't want to tell her how the TOEFL proctors had treated me. Instead, I read the entire chapter of her favourite Psalm and discovered that the verses soothed my mind as well. When Mary was asleep, I wrote a letter to the administrator asking for an explanation. I dropped by Mr. MacLeod's post office and mailed it the following morning.

In July, I passed the test and was finally able to confirm my

acceptance to McMaster University. A year later, I received a reply
from the head office of TOEFL. The letter was short, with no explanation but with a small credit for the next test, which I never used.

In June of 1989, Mother, Phổ and Phấn arrived in Canada. Her
brother Khoa helped her, bribing high-ranking officials to clear the
family's sin of trying to flee the homeland. He was able to correct the
tainted record by having Father's name and Lan Phương's removed
from the sponsorship papers. Mother brought Father's briefcase with
her, the one Phú used to drag across the floor when it was filled with
American currency. Now the riches it held were our memories of
him stressing the importance of education.

In 1991, Phổ was accepted to the University of Waterloo to study
Computer Engineering. In February of the same year, Mỹ Phương
and her family arrived in Canada. The family was finally re-united,
just as Father had wanted. That summer, on June 15, Mother held
a memorial for Father and Lan Phương. The townhouse became
crowded as all of us gathered to help Mother and Hằng Phương prepare vegan dishes.

I was in charge of the flowers for the altar. I arranged orange lilies
with white carnations and greenery in a vase shaped like a seashell.
Mother thought I would pick purple flowers and complimented
me on my choice. "Jolie, I love the combinations of the colours you
chose. Tell me why you chose lilies and carnations."

"Orange lilies express respect and honour. White carnations sym-
bolize eternal love." Years later I told her that orange lilies and white
carnations are also symbolic of deep sorrow and revitalized souls.

While waiting for the incense to finish burning, Mother asked
Phiên if he could take her to a big Vietnamese supermarket one day,
perhaps in Toronto, to find pig brains. All of us, except for Phiên,
asked the same question. "Mother, why pig brains?"

"Eating pig brains will make you smarter. My mother fed them to me before I wrote my exam."

Phiên joined in with a laugh. "When Mother bought it for us years ago, you all refused to eat it. I enjoyed it all. It was delicious, and I passed my exam the very next day."

Each year, during midterms or before final exams, Mother would search the grocery stores. "Jolie, I want to find pig brains."

"Mother, I doubt that pig brains are for sale in Canada."

Even without them, we took turns graduating and, before each ceremony, Mother would light incense on Father's altar and whisper, "Dearest husband, I am sure you are as happy as I am. It is our greatest joy each time one of our children graduates from university."

After Phấn earned his Bachelor of Science degree in the United States, Mother finally stopped asking if the supermarket carried pig brains.

CHAPTER 29

LEGACY

I was my mother's favourite child. She believed I had been blessed by our ancestors to build a good life for my family and to help my extended family prosper. She was proud that I was a filial son to her and a generous brother to my siblings. During my time in Quảng Đức, I visited her frequently, bringing her gifts of silk and other luxuries. I also used part of my wealth to build her a bigger house with more room to light incense and thank the ancestors.

She had been living with my younger brother and his family, and in her old age, her memory began to fail. Fearing for her health, Trọng Châu kept my death a secret for four years, telling her that I had reunited with my children in Canada. When she remembered, she asked my brother why she never received any letters from me, something she knew was completely out of character. A week before she passed away, she asked to return to the house that I built for her. She lit incense and prayed to hear from me; perhaps she could sense my presence. I stood beside her bed and wished I could hug her. I wanted to tell her how sorry I was that I had left this world before her. I could not finish fulfilling my responsibilities. She suddenly opened her eyes and, as our eyes met, I knew that, for an instant, she could see me. When my brother arrived the next morning, she cried and scolded him for hiding my death, telling him she could not understand what had made me go into the ocean and die with my youngest daughter. Shocked, he lit more incense and prayed for the ancestors to soothe my spirit.

My mother died peacefully three days later. She joined me in death, smiling and hugging me. She could see me fully and understood that I had left so much undone. I had chosen to remain between life and death. Moments later, I felt her embrace for the last time as her spirit rose to Heaven.

Back in Đà Lạt, during peaceful times, I installed a blackboard on a wall next to the kitchen where I often wrote a list of chores for my children to complete throughout the day. Sometimes I wrote math problems or riddles to challenge them, to remind them of the value of education.

Their learning was not confined to school. I wanted to teach them as many skills as I could. During summer vacations, I taught them carpentry skills and how to use an electric pen to burn pictures into wood. I taught them how to raise animals, to plant and grow crops and how to sew winter hats using animal fur.

Once, after the war was over, I passed around some gold ingots, carefully unwrapping their red satin cloth. I told each of my children to hold one in their hand and observe it carefully—the beautiful colour, the thin shape, the neat folds, the stamped inscription. "I know you haven't seen real gold before," I told them, "and you should see it at least once. Happiness is not decided by gold, but the world has changed, and gold may decide a human's life."

Most important of all, I tried to teach them my values. I told them stories about morality, recited traditional proverbs and took them to the temple. I taught them to honour their ancestors and appreciate their roots. Once, coming home from work, my wife and I immediately sensed an edgy atmosphere—the house was a mess, chores had not been completed and all the brothers and sisters were annoyed with each other, bickering over household tasks. I decided to use folklore to resolve their disagreements in a way that would add some fun.

That evening, during the customary family meeting, I gave each of my children a stick. "From my count, at the count of three, try to break this stick into half. Now, one…two…and three…Go!"

Each eagerly broke the stick, thinking it was a competition to see who could break it first. Then I showed them a bunch of sticks bound together. "Can you break this?"

They all shook their head, then understood my meaning. Strength lies in unity and support for each other. I recited a Vietnamese proverb: *Anh Em như thể tay chân*—brothers and sisters are like hands and legs on the same body.

I concluded with another proverb about perseverance, resilience and learning from failure: *Nước chảy đá mòn / Có công mài sắt / Có ngày nên kim*—the relentless flow of water on stone will eventually smooth out its roughness/the persistent grinding of an iron piece / with time, will turn it into a needle. Diligence is the key to success.

My flesh was present in my children; my blood flowed in them. I was proud that each of them combined analytical skills with creativity; their intelligence surpassed mine and they all possessed artistic or musical talent.

I delighted in the ways in which my daughters resembled both their mother and me. Mỹ Phương was as devoted to her children as we had been to ours, choosing to keep them safe by remaining in Vietnam despite the hardship she knew would result. Like my wife, Hằng Phương found fulfillment caring for others, hiding her compassion behind a façade of practicality. Diệu Phương inherited my spirituality, intuitively aware of the unseen world. A dreamer susceptible to extremes of joy and sorrow, she was fortunate to also inherit my wife's ability to adapt and endure.

Each of my sons prospered, reflecting a part of my character. Phiên inherited my resilience. He is like a willow tree that bends easily but is almost unbreakable. When the escape cut short his teacher training, he adapted and achieved success in a new career. Phán, also born in the year of the tiger, inherited my sense of humour and my habit of using it to camouflage serious thoughts. His personality and intelligence made him a successful project manager who excels at designing processes and leading complex teams, while Phi excels at analyzing client needs and developing appropriate solutions, just as I did for the Americans. He was also able to achieve the balance between home and career that I sought but never had the opportunity to enjoy. Like me, Phổ combined technical expertise with creativity and courage to seize an unexpected opportunity. Phấn is a careful strategist capable of envisioning future possibilities and working toward them with the same patience and diligence I put in to planning the escape.

Always the most like me, Phú is an entrepreneur at heart—a risk-taker who shared my ambition, the desire to succeed in business in a new land. He left Canada for the United States the way I left Huế for Quảng Đức. As I started my own business, so did he. He took out several patents and received multiple awards for innovation; his company was recognized as one of the fastest-growing in the US. He became a pillar for the extended family, arranging for most of his siblings to join him in California just as most of my siblings once joined me in Đà Lạt.

I was proud that my children put into practice the lessons I tried to teach them. Most of all, I was proud of their commitment to leading moral, meaningful lives. All my sons became the same filial sons to their mother that I had been to mine, and everyone assisted Phú with the charity he founded—a non-profit organization that contributes to the future of disadvantaged Vietnamese children through education. My love for them endured throughout my lifetime and beyond; through them, my legacy will live on for generations to come.

CHAPTER 30

The Net of Fate

Mother was fifty-four when Father died and she remained a widow for the rest of her life. She became very ill when she turned seventy-four; years of loneliness and sorrow had taken their toll. In 2007, Phú took her to California to live close to her sons, and she received the best medical care available. I visited her during the summer of 2010.

"Jolie, you must accept your fate," Mother said to me, lying on her hospital bed. "Fate is like a huge net that God casts out on this earth. It spreads to the end of the world, wherever you go. It covers whatever you try to do. You can never escape the net of fate." She spoke with her usual soft, sorrowful voice.

"Don't be sad anymore, Jolie. Try not to burden yourself with the deaths of your father and sister. If your father had survived, he would have spent the rest of his life plagued with sorrow, forever guilt-ridden for not being able to save Lan Phương and the many others who lost their lives."

She stayed quiet for a while, lost in memories, then continued. "A lady monk warned your father and me about his fate—if he could live past his sixtieth birthday, he would live a long life, until at least ninety. We were both young and discounted what we had heard. We did not heed the prophecy. He died when he was about to turn sixty."

What Mother said brought me back to one of our summer vacations before the end of the war. In 1973, Father drove us to a temple in Đức

Trọng, a town located about a one-hour drive from Đà Lạt. Many families visited the temple to seek a meeting with a lady monk who went by the name Bà Cha and who was renowned for her prophesies. We children played tag, running around the sanctuary grounds while Father and Mother patiently sat under a tent waiting their turn. At lunch, we were served a vegan meal. Then we were called from the playground to gather in the main hall to meet Bà Cha. She wore the usual white monk's cloak and had a white hat shaped like a turban on her bald head. She walked around us, carefully observing each child with her keen eyes. She blessed us in turn, giving each of us a copper bracelet to wear on our wrists. Father and Mother were granted a private meeting in a separate room located behind Buddha's massive white statue. They emerged a long time later, carrying with them a thick folder.

When we got home, Father labelled the folder with our pet names and locked it in a filing cabinet. The key to the cabinet was hidden in different spots; only Father or Mother had access to it. However, one time the cabinet was accidentally left open and we could not resist peeking into our files. We found that each of our profiles contained a picture of a respected elder named Ông Huỳnh Đế who was drawn in the center of the page, surrounded by an oval frame. On that frame, we each found our name located in various positions that corresponded to different body parts.

Phiên took charge, pointing out the position of our names and interpreting the meaning. He found his name near Ông Huỳnh Đế's foot. He interpreted that as a prediction that he would have to work really hard to earn his living. Phán's name was placed near the head. He would hold a management position; many people would have to listen to Phán. Phú's name was on Ông Huỳnh Đế 's hand. It was an exceptionally good position; Phú would be extraordinarily successful in anything he attempted. My name was placed on Ông Huỳnh Đế shoulder. It meant that I would have to bear a lot of burdens.

As soon as Phiên interpreted my profile, Mother caught us and was not happy that we had seen part of the predictions. Perhaps she thought it would be better if we did not know but I felt lucky that I had learned my prophecy. Otherwise, I would have wondered about it for the rest of my life. Years later, we were again able to access the cabinet, but the files were gone. Now I wondered what had happened to all our profiles.

I read pages of Buddhist scriptures so that Mother could fall asleep. She often awoke with a half-sad, half-happy smile, telling me she dreamed of Father. She saw a warm smile on his handsome face and knew it was a sign that she would join him shortly. She was happy to have a good night's sleep and dream about being reunited. Some dreams were vivid.

"Jolie, in my dream, I saw I was cooking outside, in the outdoor kitchen of our first home in Huế. Then the rain came suddenly. Your father helped me carry the small stove inside. Next, we were grocery shopping together at an outdoor market. The rain came again, and we ran to find shelter under a big umbrella, holding each other's hands. But when I looked beside me, your father was gone." Her voice was heavy with melancholy.

She showed me her half-smile again. "Jolie, in the dream, your father still looked young and handsome. I also looked young and energetic." Her tone suddenly turned bitter. "I am glad your father does not have to see me in this stage, old and frail, suffering with this awful illness."

"No, Mother. I think Father would always think you are beautiful. He would take good care of you as well."

"It is strange, Jolie. I have never heard your father say anything to me whenever I have dreams about him. But a few nights ago, in one dream, he did. It felt so real. First, he called me by my name, Sĩ. Right after that, he gave me a warm smile, then called me by the name that I liked, Ngọc."

Ngọc means precious stone and was the name she always preferred. Her tone became more cheerful. "Jolie, your father came to look for me at the hospital after we first met. My colleagues were gossiping about a handsome man who was dressed in a neat military uniform. He said he was looking for a nurse and he did not even know her name. Once I heard, I immediately knew that the gentleman was your father. Every day after that, I kept waiting to see if he would come back and he did."

Her eyes glowed for a few seconds. "Later, your father told me that he fell in love with me because of my smile."

She closed her eyes and I knew she wanted to hold on to the image of Father in her dream. Just as all of us, for the past twenty-five years, had longed to see his warm and loving smile again.

Mother passed away peacefully that summer. In her final hours, I rushed to take a flight from Ontario to California but my connection in Dallas was delayed for hours due to unusually heavy rain. Just before the plane had been about to take off, the sky had turned pitch black and the pilot had announced that we were returning to the terminal. While the sky opened up and water streamed down, I closed my eyes to pray, thinking about Mother.

I wondered if Heaven cried again as Mother passed away, while I was stuck in that airport. I needed to be by her side, seeing her half-happy, half-sad smile for the last time. I wanted to look into her eyes, eyes that had often gazed into an unknown horizon, waiting for someone who never came. I wanted to witness her joy as the years of loneliness finally ended and she was reunited with Father in a pleasant dream that no longer had to end. The parallel worlds of the living and the dead converged; Father and Mother's paths united at infinity.

CHAPTER 31
MY THIRD FUNERAL

My body stayed in Du Sinh Cemetery for twenty-nine years. More tombstones were erected. Below the hill where I lay, more streets were constructed, more houses were built and more farms were cultivated. The living continued and so did the dead.

In April of 2015, Phú sent an email to the Hoàng brothers and sisters announcing that my cremated ashes would be brought from Du Sinh Cemetery to California to be buried in the same grave as my wife.

Phán and Phổ returned to Vietnam and completed the permit to open the grave and cremate my remains, along with those of their brother and sister. They were joined by relatives, a monk and some cemetery workers. Under sunny skies, they lit incense on my grave for the last time as the monk chanted Buddhist scriptures and prayed. After that, the cemetery workers took turns digging, careful to keep my tombstone undamaged. Unlike my exhumation on Côn Sơn Island, they knew exactly what to do, and the rain did not come.

My coffin was still intact. When they opened the lid, my bones were exposed to the air for the third and final time. They were completely preserved, and the red cloth used to wrap them retained its colour and shape. I felt their tears on my bones as the two brothers embraced me, the flesh of their warm hands trembling. Then they exhumed the remains of their brother and sister; their coffins accompanied mine to a cremation centre, where my ashes were sealed in one clay urn, theirs in another.

My sons also obtained a permit for my ashes to leave Vietnam and, at Tân Sơn Nhất airport, a communist official stamped the paperwork so that, at last, I could legally leave Vietnam to enter the United States. Even so, my two sons disguised the clay urns in a royal blue carry-on bag they guarded tenderly. Like my wife and Thiện before them, they were able to board a plane without the passengers knowing they were travelling with the dead. At the airport, they asked a stranger to take a picture of them sitting on a bench with the royal blue carry-on bag between them, their hands on the bag and a smile on their faces. They sent the photo to all their brothers and sisters with a message: "Father is finally coming to America. He is flying with us on the plane, across the ocean to be with Mother!"

After thirty years, my children fulfilled my wish to reunite with them on western soil.

The urns were placed in a Buddhist temple in Orange County, California. In accordance with tradition, all my children gathered at the temple the day before the funeral, arranging flowers, cooking vegan meals and placing them besides the urns as offerings. They took turns lighting incense and praying under the guidance of the chief lady monk.

The next day, the day of my third funeral, she chanted Buddhist scriptures and arranged for all my living children to march from the temple to the cemetery. According to tradition, First Son Phiên held my picture and walked at the head of the procession. Behind him, Third Son Phú carried my ashes. Beside him Second Son Phán carried the ashes of Phu and Hồng Phương. The rest of my children walked behind them, each carrying flowers and incense. The monk led the funeral march along a path lined with palm trees to the burial spot.

The breeze carried the salty scent of the Pacific Ocean to the cemetery, bringing with it the memory of Lan Phương, whose body dissolved in the Pacific Ocean. The sky was blue, decorated with a few floating clouds. This time, the only rain came from tears. The monk chanted more scriptures and blessed the burial site. Each child in turn placed their hands on the clay urn that contained my ashes, fulfilling my wish to embrace each of them again. Finally, my ashes were lowered into the ground next to my wife, our souls intertwined as one.

Third Daughter, Diệu Phương lit a cigarette, my favourite kind, Craven A, and placed it on top of the fresh soil. The lady chief monk stood beside her and said, "Diệu Phương, last night, I had a dream. In the dream, I saw three playful children at this burial site, a boy and two girls."

"That must have been Anh Phu, Em Hồng Phương and Em Lan Phương."

My soul wandered among the living for thirty years. I saw it all, from the moment I left my children fatherless, to the moment they matured. I felt it all, from the moment my family was divided to the moment we were re-united and my children finally let me go. At last, I could embrace my dear wife, the love of my life. Fate cut our love short; now our souls would be together forever.

God appeared before me and re-opened the door of Heaven. I held my wife's hand and we walked through together.

Dear God—In my next life, please let me be my father's daughter again.

Author's Note and Acknowledgements

As I completed this book, I also marked twenty-five years of teaching as a college mathematics professor. While sorting through my old university textbooks, I came across a poem and a paragraph that I had scribbled beside the formulas and challenging calculus problems, along with repeated question marks. Writing is a concealed passion that has patiently waited for the right time to reveal itself. Solving mathematical problems has kept my mind stay in focus, but writing has detangled the maze of unanswered questions. As I struggle in life, I learn that new sorrows trigger old wounds, and words have the power to heal.

I am indebted to many—

My parents, brothers and sisters for your immense love and for sheltering me, especially my brother Hoàng Trọng Phú for your wisdom. I am thankful for the many conversations that we had during the intense writing months. You were the first to read the complete original draft. I am grateful for your kind words of encouragement and generous compliments about my writing.

My daughters, Helen, Christie and Charlotte, and my grand-children, Cora and Oliver, for filling my life with joy, happiness and never-ending love. A special thank you to Christie and Charlotte for their aesthetic illustrations for the book cover and the interior.

217

My editors, Lynn Duncan and Kilmeny Jane Denny, for polishing my writing. I am deeply grateful for your patience and your professionalism.

The next generations of the Hoàng family, including nieces, nephews, grandnieces and grandnephews: this book is the answer to questions about your roots, about the enduring love and the immense sacrifice that your grandparents gave to your parents.

Lastly, I am grateful to Judy and John Smith, the founders of The Mountain Fund to Help the Boat People. When you wrote our names on the sponsorship paper, you gave us a country, a future and completed our freedom.